from stone this *running*

by Heller Levinson

BLACK
WIDOW
PRESS

Boston, MA

from stone this *running*

by Heller Levinson

Black Widow Press is an imprint of Commonwealth Books, Inc., Boston, MA. Distributed to the trade by NBN (National Book Network) throughout North America, Canada, and the U.K. All Black Widow Press books are printed on acid-free paper, and glued into bindings. Black Widow Press and its logo are registered trademarks of Commonwealth Books, Inc.

Joseph S. Phillips and Susan J. Wood, Ph.D, Publishers
www.blackwidowpress.com

Cover Design: Kerrie Kemperman
Typesetting: Kerrie Kemperman
Cover Art: detail of *Linen Drawing, III*
               Linda Lynch, 2007
               Oil on linen, 26 x 30"
               Courtesy of the Artist

ISBN-13: 978-0-9837079-5-0

Printed in the United States

10 9 8 7 6 5 4 3 2 1

ACKNOWLEDGMENTS

The author would like to express his deep gratitude to the following magazines (both print and online) in which some of these applications have previously appeared or will be appearing:

Alligatorzine, Blue and Yellow Dog, The Cartier Street Review, Counterexample Poetics, ditch poetry, First Literary Review-East, Jacket, Mad Hatters' Review, Mad Swirl, Mid-June, Omega, Otoliths, Poets for Living Waters, Skidrow Penthouse, Street Cake Magazine, Sugar Mule, Talisman, Tears In The Fence (UK), The Toronto Quarterly, A Trunk Full of Delirium, Venereal Kittens, and *Wood Coin.*

Additionally, special thanks must go to both Victoria Ganim and Mary Newell, whose contributions to the construction of this manuscript have been invaluable.

for Clayton Eshleman

WHEN

WEEP,...

is all
that is left

MODULES

FROM _____ *THIS* _____

IN THE _____ *OF* _____

_____ *L I K E* _____ _____

THE ROAD TO _____ *ROAD*

WITH

WITH _____ THIS _____

SMELLING

MODULAR MODIFICATION

FUSION RECONNOITER

Individual Application:
in the sonic of stone ¤ 161

Fusion:
sonic like altitudinous skin
    reconnoiters
        in the sonic of stone ¤ 162

THE FECUNDATING ROTATIONAL CLUSTER

The Interfecundating Rotational Cluster Collusional

Hinge Tabulatories

Placement

INTRODUCTION

from stone this running represents the second Hinge Enactment (following *Smelling Mary*, HDP, 2008).

The Hinge Universe has been developing since *SM* and the 'outposts' in this volume represent these new inclusions. For those new to Hinge who reflexively ask, "What is it?" I'd like to respond by excerpting from Jared Demick's interview in *The Jivin' Ladybug*, where he asks just that.

Jared: In ten words or less, can you describe Hinge? How is Hinge different from other methods of poetry-fashioning?

James: ...Well, part of the beauty of Hinge Theory is that I always say it is non-reducible,—i.e. non-shelvable, commodifiable, label-able. So my ten-word-or-less answer for what is Hinge, is the following: It's not what it Is, but how it Behaves. There—nine words—whew! When people used to ask me what Hinge was, I'd beg my publisher, Michael Annis (Howling Dog Press), to hurry up and produce the book, *Smelling Mary,* because then I could answer them with "Here" (giving them the book). "Here is Hinge." That would be the one-word answer—"Here." And of course, now, with *fstr,* we have further elaboration/amplification/extension. Another—"Here." For those seeking additional discussion and clarification, please visit: http://tinyurl.com/heller-levinson. Also, Michael Annis's astute Hinge Manual is indispensable for a fuller grasp and appreciation: http://issuu.com/howlingdogpress/docs/the_hinge_manual___related_criticism.

SM sprung forth four modular developments. *fstr* continues with modular development, as well as offering modular mutations, or, in some cases (as with 'placement'), breeding entirely new formulations. While greeting new awarenesses and stirrings, this introduction also seeks to identify those continuously arising perplexities—'perplexities' guised as the most enchanting and seductive *curiosities.* One such curiosity is what I shall term modular velocity.

Modular Velocity

is the notion that each module supports an integral velocity factor. An example of this *curiosity* is that the "from ____ this" module and the "with ___ this" module were initiated at approximately the same time, yet, a far greater number of particles/applications (at the time of this writing, 24 to 6) were sprung from the "from/this" module than from the "with/this" module. Why is this? Is the Linguistic Tissue, the Word-Chemistry, the Modular Combustibility of one module that much at variance with that of another? Is it the fertility factor of the particle being submitted? Would there be twenty-four alternative particles that would favor being sprung from a "with/this" module? Is there an actual chemistry to the word, the module, that creates a distinct frisson, a definitive ignition? Can this attraction be specified? A delineation mapped out that would designate certain words/particles to certain modules and other particles to others as not all sperms and eggs fertilize?

Or is the variance a function of the Hinge Practitioner? Might another practitioner have placed the same particle placed in the "from/this" module into a "with/this" module? And what would that subjective bent reveal?

We observe that we are at the borderline: at a locus in our explorations that demands we view language as biology, as chemistry, as a realm of reproduction.

Another curiosity/perplexity is what we shall term the migratory.

Migratories

are elements in an application that fructify through further contexts. It varies from an EED[1] by not being a modular construction. It can be a word that has reverberated in other applications or a cluster of words. It can be a grammatical device, a signature, a signification, or any gesture that emboldens through gustoing perambulatory urge. These roaming 'elements' behave like warp yarns shuttling—*threading*—Revelatory Infections. It is an area to watch.

Hinge Propagatory

refers to the nature of Hinge to produce practitioners, as well as artistic events. Hinge Lightning has struck numerous souls and I shy away from citing names for fear of

---

[1] EED = Embedded Explosive Device. See 'Placement' outpost. Examples of both an EED and a Migratory can be found in the application "with blade this into." The EED is "the road to necessary road," and the migratory is "edge as departure," a word cluster arising from the application "from sharpening this edge." To enrich one's appreciation of "with blade this into," it is appropriate to visit both applications to experience the accumulative resonance.

omitting those already practicing, as well as neglecting those set to commence. I feel we are on the ground floor of developmental material that is cataclysmic in its reach, intent, and import. A warm welcome and embrace to all participants.

Modular Multipliers

Creating new modules is a requirement for enriching the Hinge Universe. Because each Module tosses the particle[2] into a particular environment (ether), maximum enrichment entails that each particle be submitted to as many modules as possible. Thus, Particle Densification relies on a rich Modular Spectrum.

The new modules arising in *fstr* are the following: with ___ this ___; from ___ this ___; a two-syllable word, plus "like," followed by either a three- or four-syllable word, and ending with a one-syllable word, i.e., – "clumsy like meandering salt."[3]

---

[2]   For readers unfamiliar with this terminology, please see Appendix I.

[3]   The "like" application, "love like apparitional joinery," has a three-syllable ending and represents syllabic shifts as a fertile area for extended modifications of this module.

FROM _____ THIS _____

FROM ARSON THIS CHAR

the singe arcane with reference
bounty a pilfer percolate destitute
premeditation a railroad a runaway a deliberation striking
.....
palette revision
a vision
casting

FROM EQUIPOISE THIS TRAIN

        (L train, 14th Street Canarsie Line
leech lurch   (larch) rattle
clacket
        metal
        brakery
inferno designed lighting
inferno guest list
scythe risible   black yellowing teeth magnified (growing (sharpening
((pincering
a boom room tomb room
a clutch of demise
the earthiness under the earth   under(n)ea(r)th
beneath – brook stepping   (poise
               critical

> If you lost an itch in the subway or bus
>
> visit our New Lost & Found Website

breach broach reproach   brook no
allowance   allowan(ces)
faces a repulsion shrine

going to: vehicles take you there, conveyances (wrapp(e)(ntombe)d in), contain-
    ments, contaminants—en-clo-*sures,* brooking *no open* .....
tracks take you there   tracking (a trail (trailing (tail (tailing (*behind* the scent
    object? [train scent [training scent] (staying on track (staying on track gets
    you there — arrival (arriving at, ... to appear, upon arrival destination *appears,*
occurs   with occurrence
destination *arrives*   →→→→→ fulsome
                        fulgent

sulphurous
divagate ://: [4] navigate
brooks & the function of in(de)cline
flat surfaces facilitate the laying of track
lumbering the *out-lay*

m(a)e(t)tering a calibration of
a way to climate
the perspiration of things
                            (alternate ending)

perspiratives

---

[4]   See Appendix II.

lame wrack   r(j)ustification
    wood burn   < mood barn >   forest furnace flame
refuge fugue figuration fortify fortification
  —Anselm Kiefer   Chaim Soutine –
        ↕   ↕
      ∟ their woods ⌐
    preservation woodshed burn away
burning wood mind kindle in the grip the gripping
exercising matter exorcising matter the + p(l)ush (flush crush)[5]
of tracking tabulating is a bicycle too preferences do for what to burn wood or
fiber, cotton say, plastic reeks a hypnotic choreography has the appease of *trans*-
figuring combustion can be accidental or prescribed the prescription is reckoning
& encourages recall
the
maximum flammable

---

[5] " +" before a word indicates the parentheticals may serve as substitutes/alternates, as a fused add-on (an entirety), or in any combination that the reader finds most satisfactory.

A nod to Emily Dickinson.

FROM GALLOP THIS BOGART[6]

image heist/hoist   haul
conditioning the perceptual highway   highjack
highjacking the occipital cortex
a retinal holdup
a shootout

occlusive eye
eyeball coercion
eyesore

Cinema means pulling a uniform over our eyes, warned Kafka,
wearing the threads of another man's image –

shoplifting light
light baronial & baryonic
vermicular strike
light analyzed as supine

the consensual nature of image – [the imagistic survival system (to trace the perception of an image over time ... its endurings, its mutations)] – narratives adhering through syphilitic dams, the image intact, integral, swimmingly afloat –
Bogart Blooms

::: how would we decode an image? deformulate? if we stopped a frame during a screening, and wired the audience so that each person could recreate that frame as they imagined, how many differing frames/images would we receive? what would they look like? what would they tell us? :::

to rope the retinal renegades
with their unreeling revealings
reel real feel → peel the reel
a reeling I will go – *heigh ho!*
wheeling color chromium nitrate cluster globule counterfeit straw syllogistic fresh
pistil pilings schism maw

---

6   Eadweard Muybridge – often called the Father of the Motion Picture – developed photographic techniques to show sequential movement in order to settle Leland Stanford's $25,000 bet that at some point during a horse's gallop all four hooves are off the ground at once.

celluloid seal/sealant
spooling time's stitchery
cognizance:
successions – *image pile-up* – integrated ↔ the great lob of thickening →
accumulating correspondences → identity emerges from integrations
    → integration a function of correspondence ∓
correspondence   alightment   allotment

to *see* past/through (Passin' thru = Charles Lloyd, Gábor Szabó, Chico Hamil-
ton)/over & around the construction

the film star as Star as luminosity polluting the night
        dark extermination

seedlings ↔ purse → reed
remonstrance
illumination = vision
=
trance-misting

clippety harbor shortage   JuniorharpspeakWells
churl delicious   free fall   trump bullion lanyard bask brilliant
freckling the
book satchel fresh bath(ed) boiling pumps petticoats no pettifoggery flirty
skirty me so(a)/r/(u)le yr feet me roughage yr plumage

dedicated pitch canister breath cups to daisy cluster the eyebrow wand lip
truculence sweet gardenia accommodation accelerating Mustang overhorsepower
load   load up on ....

"can I go home wit' you
Tell yo' mama and yo' papa
Lord, I'm a lil schoolboy too"

... unload
oooh oooh Eeeeeh
fructose fantail flush flesh pharmaceuticals
mango electric sugarplum armpits brow of lunacy delirium shoulders sweet
derriere lollipop billow the swallow of tambourine shingles curly my burly burrow
braidings willow paradings swillow misting mystify pillow your must

electric liquefaction riverlick sorbet
                    s-c-r-e-a-m

holler in the crystalline flame of the *Out-Pour!*

FROM GRACE THIS AMAZING

..... excrescence
crustacean claw   egret pines storm
the constables regulatory blind   a sky
faint of wheeze
the fish no longer nasty
dispositionality meshes to homocercal security

whereabouts is the plane of treaty
entreating enterprise stakes bullion bulldozery move over
stars bloodied by lame guitars
the song the wolf
lowering
to scent

leviathan ranges steaming
the whales
       —arch locomotives
       —aerial adjutants
rumble through green gateways puckering garner
gabling odontecete risings purling pastures weeping therapeutic silence

aqua combings   syllabi rewritings
days no longer injurious but supplicant
envious of wind traffic & eager for contraband the skiff wardens calibrate glass

cloak uprising
cruising magisterial Harleys sputtering breath declare
"now is the last alert"
the long lumberings jeopardized the crazed gymnastic cleat splashes *g-l-a-z-e* the
twisted dashes the fin fantailing lobpeppering frisk-dives depleting

now
pitched to a bravura coloratura
scorching the fathoms with wrack lament
these monks of the deep
              winching helium clairvoyance
enlist fox & sea horse   gorilla & chimpanzee
        zebra & bobcat

these underlyers ://: overseers
collect plasma-sets/pith-posses/deft marauders
fluke deserts mountains lowlands mesas hills & trough
sanctify blowhole
    the upright bass
    coltshooves searing
    syncopation
    wild manes sweeping cerebral spheres

these swashbuckle prophets
claw final scripture to outlaw
    unmusical barleys   vanishing vocabularies
drought chalk   stapled rhythm
                dead tongue

with eyes seeing since the upper Cretaceous
70,000,000-year-old eyes
eyes long looking
lashing the *continuously initial*
"But the whaleman, as he seeks the food of light, so he lives in light."

so the whale
lives in light & no light

FROM HANDS THIS GUITAR

arc funding utter
 —libretto arch
[11/29/08   107 Broadway
        Guitarists
  Joe Giglio/John Stowell]
attack   settle
scrum ambush volley   rivulet rue
the fire next time
scatting Satin Doll press Blakey roll blasts careen cylindrical pistol bricolage pops
                              lambent tango reed sustain Satie drips
                                      serried ruminants
rapid fire ascension transportationals   seaweed drift skirt folds meditation
moss
                                              ferrying breakwater
        b(g)lade s(t)urf runner c(g)lad (light)ning breather
{Lesion: the fifth string of Joe's Forshage Clownfish Ergonomic and the first
string of John's SoloEtte quit their guitars. The players remark, are non-plussed.
The strings tangle and cavort. Divide and sub-divide – four strings, eight, sixteen,
form into hands, shadow the player's hands, elongate into pure fingers, *imagine
music without fingers, champion fingers* – recollect – eight, four, two: Music is a
collectivizing and divisionalizing of tones. Can there be an occupation with no
occupier? The absence on the fretboard. Coming to this absence. With aptitude,
with ammunition. Migrating this space to purly allocatives ravenous with gypsy
garish whorl dress churn. Session: the strings return—enlivened from exploring
the prehistory of sound—settle & attune.}

    The Hand is a meditation upon design.

        Embraceable You
          four handed lunge
        white Percherons carriaging tune
          embracing a tune
          embarking upon a tune
            —tune-*full*   *full-filling*

tune   attune-*ment*   adjustment ://: augment
            Joe/John
perfervid robust lasso leaps spur placement perfidy city boulder mass transversible
pasta breach

                              succor carousels ... pink flamingos
carpentry Camargue stallions
              (rouse) ambulan(ce)t ruse
        {the spine connects the brain to nerves in the hand}
Pollock splash Klein swipes   El Greco   Picasso
                              Blue Guitar
                      Rothko pastel sleights
                              (sleddings
        thi(e)s(e) hand(s)   thi(e)s(e) guitar(s)

            Con
            —Versions

            the
            In
            Contro
            Vertible

FROM HORSE THIS BRAND

> "I'm gonna catch that horse if I can
> And when I do I'll give her my brand"
> —The Byrds, "Chestnut Mare"

looping over   en(sorcell)circling the neck
                                                (attributional
ensorcery (ell)   → corralling   —"I'll give her my brand and we'll be
friends for life just like a wife"   huntspeak: to bag to bring down
marking territory   remarking   remarkability
possession is a bringing closer? a bringing into? a taking in, to enlarge?
a proximity to amplify?
I've got my brand on you
mine
what's mine is mine
mining the mine mindfield
in the branding of horse the brander seeks pacification

domesticity
the truant

FROM HORSE THIS MERMAID

skin-slick Godiva stride saddling stallion ride girt   alabaster/flesh
flesh atop Corot white   rubescent locks flicker   dart
colors spooling   hue-pools drift mingling
collaboratives   mercurial swamp slag – *mélange mesmerisms*
    cannon/shin hoof/foot
        school flexions
leg spills   luscious root lures   luring
succulence drips   trot-hot   launch haunch hunching
spherical hoists
lolls of bob-festering
        —caprice snags
        —coital squirms
festivaling to sea
        —pelagic grabs
        —salinity spills
drilling liquescence
celestial rubs
      welling
wings
tail

FROM HORSE THIS SADDLE

seat ...
an adder-ing   atop   elevation
[hierarchical steer   ]   a surmise
overview → overseer → overseeing
                                   {perspectival saw
mount   mounted   mountain   mountainous
                 {high up
overlook   lookout   outlook
a superlative
:// : separate the bird from its feet
    perpetual flight ://:
a proposition above an outlook
propositions require outlook
to outlook/lookout is to propose
lookout for the outlook of the proposition
propping up   saddle props
an upward station
is a saddle an outlook
what does it propose
is it a proposition
what is its outlook

FROM LOQUACIOUS THIS EASEL

westward drill
intent with summons
counterfeiting larkspur melodies
numinous geographies

deploring
the low ground
canvas misfirings
pigments mistressing
ignorant of station

(containerships necklace the seas
    —bleed matriculates

banking pneumatic corollas
hilariate
windspray vineyards
the trump magnificence of sunsledding overlords

brushstrokes
defiant
hemotrophic
fat
with color

FROM LUST THIS WANDER

wanderlust   roam loam
lyricism
abutment
stir-things

travel as an amendment
as prescriptive emanation
a flow-flaw
fragility
flummery

lines of deposit
conveyance

FROM MERMAID THIS SNAKE

winch ... slink   surplus unerring
query: an appendage in atrophy
efficiency: suppling   a *wind-up*
Mami Wata[7] snake issues
to bind her catch   to waylay   to
man-tie

overhead snake twirl this oceanic cowgirl
this reptilian empress   queen of the lanyard crunch
tosses lariats venom-laced or
fecund – catch depending—their teeth, their caliber, their inundator

horizon replete giddy scooters a cowgirl ambush
cheerleaders for world hygiene   this
estuarial caucus   threaded chiasmus elope   claw looses legions rumbles
precipice quiddity press
cow punchers   belt dazzlers   winding through the winds of a trafficking
necrosis
giddyup springs   crocodile waterfalls   canine cathedrals
waterswells of salubrious posse sprawl the land
a hirsute hybrid collective
springy, credit worthy
combustible, cagey
 a launch of siren decibels   honey vowels
seething molecular jungles
a riptide of talent scouts
strung like a rainbow of hawks
as the lasso coursed the west
these succulent snake charming sweethearts swirling their saurian daughters
.....
draw

---

[7]   African water spirit.

FROM MERMAID THIS TAIL

bespook   bedazzling   jewel
ing   jeweled .....
token to epidermis & calligraphy
cartography & pulse   testimonial
terse   lore trove   trophy froth
in the bed of sapience a spear
probing   penetrative
pierce

from preposition to *par*-ti-cle
groove time
from delivery to happenstance
spoon train
rail spray convexity root swim snare press *r-o-o-lll* Lee Morgan unleashed
launched spit forth struck → *Outward* lavish tonguings (doubletriple) airtake
valvular hyperventilative lavish lunging lungy rimshot pip-snap pop incantatory
contagious bandit storms
                                                              [stagecraft
→→ ⌂∂ △
Art Blakey
progenitor   generator   generations*generating*
                                              [beget begin
spinning → Bobby Timmons, Lee Morgan, Johnny Griffin,
Wayne Shorter,   , a hotbed BlakeyUniversity breeding grounds   a fern hill
orgasmic fructuous fleshpot Ferris wheelin fiesta hive
.....   armadillo trots
glandular grabs   saddle sores
ΔΔ⌂ ⌂ ΔΠΣ ∩∩ ∩ ΔΔΔΔ   Δ
with

Blakey, ... A Night In Tunisia
sound pound bound rumble gourd ground
bean bursts bubble boasts primed Serengeti interval drills
          click clock   heaping swarms of polyrhythmic magma swamp swills
, cymbal clarion calls   stratospheric crash whoops
Whorl Whorl   Hoo Hooooo
Voodoo Vandals   trumpet screech moan ploan pilot trumpet
tome   foundry bulldoze furnace bramble franchise hose moss milkweed mink kit-
tens =======
        unfurlin surfin hazard in the lollipopin lollapalooza cruller atoll roiling
raillery raze luminosity arch syncopation temblor sympathetic loll   caw zone loan
a'blazin
sticks a'lickin luxury timer
the mothership

collectivizing
alimentar -i- ventili – fi – cation
—*ing*

FROM PLANT THIS RIBBONING

fraternity   the demiurge
mute, cathartic ... spindling coincidentals
a breath of particle   with rhythm
          particle breach
conditioning seek with smooth
inquisitive circumferences the labor involved
fetching forward –
wayward
ward of the way
plan plant planted plantation planeterium plane pathology planner planing a plan
planch ....
....
plucking deliberations
tying wood

FROM RUNNING THIS ISSUE

issuance   insinuation   inSur-ance
    forth   bring forth   +froth (broth trough)
coax   coaxial   alignment
[foaming] [beaming]   a rudder by
tabernacle   traction   paladin
                        sail forth

go

this admission. valves   formation   routings

a summons   pour through   a pouring
a celebration on the peduncle of flamboyance
cataract rebound developed to fit the horse
              —{a sing through}—
symbiosis of ride of ridership of the
announcement that pronounces
                              [to think through
                               branch(ing)(e)(s)
                              [to denude
                                  consideration
flowthrough
outpour
respire   saxophone://:lung
                  reed://:lung   reed://:tongue
              saxophone://:tongue saxophone://:reed

tongue lung lung tongue
                      —lunge
lunge lung tongue   / hung
saxophone a lung
breeze a lung
breezin
lungin

Note: The fourth line, "... to fit the horse," refers to the fact that Adolphe Sax designed the saxo-
phone so that it could be played by a soldier while riding a horse. Sax felt that the military orches-
tra could improve its musical power with the addition of that specially designed instrument.

geometry   metrics
              blade
to cut

cut   up
cut   through
                              (cutthroat)
        slice dice chop
dissect   parse   parsnip   pursed
    "A sharpening steel's purpose, therefore, is to push back the blade's
        teeth so they stand up and cut again. In this sense, a sharpening
        steel doesn't actually sharpen it; it just realigns or 'hones' the edge."[8]
"refresh" buttons reestablishment
activity establishes reestablishes
fire: shape modifier
modification a constant
                    carbon clad boogie spheroidal bop
cut-ups cute
circulating chromatic seizures
cutting into (tooth/claw) essential for sustenance
eviscerate
establishing/creating edge
a leadership role – cutting edge
edge as departure point*
as point of confrontation → cutting
into
consider the edge of the cut object
consider being without an edge, borderless
, borderless being?
being at the edge → precipice, falling [see *above
the knife edge is sharpened to facilitate invading another edge

---

[8]   "Sharper," by Todd Oppenheimer (*The New Yorker,* Nov. 27, 2008).

the knife, then, as a traveler

→ a border crosser

: vegetables as a highway system ("We'll be passing through tomato.")

sharpening:

a velocity function

FROM TAIL THIS MERMAID

outgrowth   pour   outpour
flush   creation   phantasmagoria
password

configuring from
arrangement this daunt

FROM THROAT THIS HORSE

runic creamery   an
articulation outpouring   the
speech infinitudes

FROM VULVA THIS WORMHOLE

allotment ...
bust escape alacrity velocity placement constitutionals
zonage perplexity a value a value system a
valuation .....
the laity is imperfect
madmen mossed in vulva hive
redistribute their incomes

parsimony legal   blunt instruments
both hammer & stun   this is not
a debatable duct
                    {I hacked my way out –
                        {premature birth was their expression
vulva is the lack that plenishes
                            {good sex, unlike a good meal, is inefficient ...
                                {it leaves you wanting more
vulva→ transversible wormhole
        reversible
        convertible
        preferred debt obligation

the plunge that quickeneth
& in the hour of my need
the dispatch the displacement   the disbursement

from perplexity this riddle
how the is of the is is the not that is not is
the impossibility of plotting both the velocity of prick & location of prick at the
same time
wherewithal   epistemology
applying for a research grant as: the first menstruating penis
cross-bordering
studying enlargement: container contains

the contained-in ... concatenate
corridors of preemption//mix
lost in the lost
wading in
attribution

FROM WINDINGS THIS PURSE

a predisposition to sound the horn
collectivizing a stirment mapped by gurney
this trot undergoing meter & space
loosen the strings

IN THE _____ OF _____

IN THE AGE OF EDGED WEAPONS

cut!   cutlery capsules crull the crepuscular oblong
incision redecorating
the slash of proximity knowing your neighbor
breed warts
designing an allocation process cowardice
is the clock ungainly ring time
TO T(H)RUST is
TO BE a Duane Reade Club Card Reject
in an age of
Age Defying Moisturizers
honor demands it the blade expands ...
frolicsome the punch is long
overdue & who wouldnt for sex
has the capacity to be the non-
deliberable in a world gone
pointed objects
piercing

IN THE BANDAGE OF MUMMY

alleviate   rinse :// : rising
angulation   stir   tempo-mold
texture :// : contextual
packaged prurient
rami - fi - ca - tions
ram - i - fy
no holds barred
trespass
a merely

IN THE BRANDING OF HORSE

claim, ... claimant
                    (*saturant roundup*
corral   looping the neck ringing
the finger
        "She'll be just like a wife"
establishing intimacies
does the tattoo attach us to ourselves
does being inside the other bring us the other
in branding do we place ourselves

reining in
ropes
conversation encircling

IN THE COMBING OF SILENCE

fanfare   relegation   regulation   regis
tra   tion
cornerings, drift
geometries
direction
follow the hairline

IN THE DELAY OF TRACTABLE

The helplessness of human young... in the long run redounded in truly extraordinary fashion to the advantage of mankind. It opened wide the possibility of cultural as against merely biological evolution. Cultural evolution became the means whereby the human animal despite his unimpressive teeth and muscles, rose to undisputed pre-eminence among the beasts of prey. —William H. McNeill

retardation blossoms
                        fecund marinate
slow slake   snake compos(ure)ition
snow dogs accelerate reptilian sunrises
stillborn the moors
masks mitigant
management cranky with procedure
experimentation leaky
rapidity feints emergence
a gravitational bluff

IN THE DEPOSITORIES OF TALE

constellative slime   a slime that settles that
fills in   allegiances bind to the
rediscovered
reckonings
anthems
hostings & beckons
wellsprings

land
gathering

IN THE HOL(Y)(INESS)DING OF MERMAID

... wet
a slime of skin
a constellative reconstituting
the constitutionality of contact
conduit   border crossing
currency traffic   net affiliatives   a consideration
consider-*ing*
suspension-crackling
space opportunes protrusion pills a coax collage
entranc-*es*
latitudinal rinse
threshing altitudes

IN THE HULL OF BAREBACK

lingering smoke from a retrolingual squall
scrambling grammar perfervid
tambourine smacking imps outwitting the oversized

through a prehistoric snorkeling subdividing breath
the
New Speech
speaking of augment & wander
bristling new harmonies in the dark ear of the crow
measuring panther by wind

across this salinity divide
hide strophing the great white of the plains
banking to the breeze of an incalculable wonder
an eruption of tone resembling a maturating pinto
a stride like an ancient command
repeating

IN THE IN OF LOVE

in love   love-in   lov-ing   ingin
in-ing   inning   innings of love
...
begin begun   beginning innings love begin-ings
in tin pin kin sin fin love of the in
incretionary incunabula incantatory incandescent indescribably indecent infiltra-
tive love
in-**fes**-ta-*tive*
in—out   out & in   inoutoutinoutinin
vin
akin
with love
begin

IN THE IS OF IS-ING

is is

IN THE SACK OF CURL

plangency   peals from a
water scar
drought-dread dungeon dare down
dark darling
strick
sulk platoons
ribbon nonce
sallies careened, stipulated, ... jeopardized
low fibrillative

canny caulking   shoulder wake
   permission slips
  {the wing is the aureole of climate}
paw cleat
path along the ground
sessile pour   fit espy
    flexion loose
     anatomical algebra
      herd cleanser
Canis Lupus through the woods
       memory wag
shimmering whale skein metrics a species of
breathtaking
cirrus lo(e)co(ny)m(m)(y)otion
   strip intervals
     drift coalescement
svelte insertion a clause boulder wiggling
a steaming brush-stroking psychic crawler triggering archaic shutdowns
       —mammalian moth
this pack packed intention
limb toboggans
circulates

IN THE WING OF MONGOLIAN EAGLE

resource, ...   loft
caucus   blither
perspiring equinoctial gales burble eyeball gallops gutter updraft fiesta jubilee
sprees ......
hammocking solar clumps   a rouse
of ocean harps swiggle sea shells
                                    the spell
of lore   of rumors shuttling

...
venous trapezoid   mnemonic trapdoor
catch & carry
intermingling celestial sportster
                                    lung caster

frolicking glyph spreader
runic brooder
gliding crotch thistle accelerator craft
posting
            &
seer - *ing*

_____ _LIKE_ _____ _____

ARSON LIKE DISTRIBUTIVE BRONZE

mitts empty enmity celerity toss
rush burn brite ripover rake
avaricious crawl
cretaceous warbler
imminent dissembler rage loquacious liquidity lyre
luxuriant odalisque panting
consuming to illuminate to fire
rilling drills from loquacious lyre fibrillate fruits
cutaways cull brim fountains dancing shoeless migrations
makeover tides
alterations tailor
delinquent scribbler
reconfiguration plot

CHATTER LIKE BANALITY FLUSH

like a species of subtropic malodor
a lamentation stitched with stale fish
a subsidy recall
a tongue warted with squamous intestine

sundays burp delirium tremens
subways troll for a dependable provider
reflex persiflage inundation capillary bewitch
the hook-ups are failing
ringworm tapes the filing systems puckers the observational towers
ceremonies tumbling down
the spectacle jettisons glamour,
rescinds, ... a slow deflation
connectivities splinter the gap gapens
void maw
chlorophyll modalities in default
plenish :// : penury
the sentence sharp & sudden

CLUMSY LIKE MEANDERING SALT

posted in dehydration   liabilities
cherish the inadequacies of measurement
strike a new pose
sponsor a drummer reluctant to leave his tom tom
the sort that yanks apostrophes into contented commas
that learns the balance beam the gymnastics of conjure
spread across the palette of traffic signals
the even beats
under the spell

COMBING LIKE PERFIDIOUS BURST

unrule   tangle   rinse &
towel dry   notions   style
as desired ...

....

assortment   parts   concerns
relegate   regulate   reliqua(ry)-ation
wayward-ness
plausibility pawns pursue puerility plaudit prostrate prong particular, please
a persuasion   a look   a gel
a resistance
pertinence pithing

HORSE LIKE OUTPOURING CRANE

winged temperature
a blood panel drilling loft
the bemusement of flight
    (conditionality a dejection trigger?
    (the library systematizing wrecking the dialogue the first breach?
contemplation aerializing thermals
Hushing the Eocene with spectacle
frosting the pugnacious
furtherance
trapeze   spring
likelihood

JOINTURE LIKE ALACRITY PLANE

vessel – ing   Tongue & groove   vehemence
velocity chute   channel
a disposition   channeling disposition
adjunct/assemblies
                           (cryogenic purse
capitulation the erotic pedestal pedal
ling   through time globes   eras
of swamp fuss
of glaciations

                    — — —

.....

stitchery

LAMENTATION LIKE INGLORIOUS SILK

souring inventory depletion   the old man
stands before the subway station fidgeting with
his Ziploc bag

bag
to hold
to contain

sweltering carp belly up
holding swelter
          burning carp

pilla(o)ry toil
the steps   that g(wr)e(ck)t   you there
      —wreckage that spills
      —a wrecking-flow
wreck reeking rudderless   careen down
lonely street   the t(h)orn garden the
landscape that t(j)e(ers)ars   umbrage &
saltpeter
pilot systems that descry the shallows
the mandible that winked   a reconnaissance referral
a way out
din

fusion blossoms   fructuous spears   replete piercings
hinging weather systems spool overlap unison merge
... erge urge purge converge courage cover-*age*
tools usage forge together ensemble bring
rummaging armies escorting a congress of organs
in avowal ......
coax crest prehensile loan behest
splitting   partitioning   adjournment
a tremulous colossal   pinions & rack   attunement
tuning: intervals/unisons   steps: taken/abandoned
          forthwith ://: foresaw
tuning—an anointment; an assembling of parts; a pathway, a
– virt-u-osity
                  pitch pouring
              unison froth
              fractal fever

an octave
gathering

MERMAID LIKE RECALCITRANT THRUSH

oblong belonging genus barefisted siren song sling branchfinning trance spun
postal clocks leaf the forest
transportation is the song's rebuttal
the horizon in capsize
eggshelling architect's with caprice
what is architecture but the endeavor to formulate form   with
bump as alterior extenuation   as device that falters
& urges   that primitive early zone   the zone eliding time's approval
where fin was capital & crown
slithering through sects of withholding
dispatching black patches
for vision

OUTLAW LIKE APPARITIONAL FLAW

diadem drift the loss is law ...
clear-sighted range operatives employing the latest in
smile sensitive technologies post obliquities
on raw angulations
installing alertness in the courtyards summons
the scruffy & the lame the lupine valves
lump a witness orgasm program recursive with
stopgap   instruct the storefronts to exercise
wily the illusory napkins are well-pitched no longer surly
the getaway is
Seduction
&
North

PALTRY LIKE ECUMENICAL FLESH

reams of canvas broth luffing
lapse time temporals achieve
a sitting position
the other side of otherness
is other
departments of _____
in correctional facilities one learns
the movementworthy in stun,
the measurements necessary to fold
a shipwreck
hears liquidity

PITHING LIKE ADMIRALTY BURST

shelling   shocking
shell schlock shock shekels
shelling smelling dwelling welling
a four-star flag officer scything the seas
rilling the deep under abuse over shoulder boards binding
molasses conferring with excitable Torpedo rays
the doctrine of equivalence is undergoing a replacement
in manners while crystals skirt bellies of foam   foreclosures
float the land   delirial free-fall spasmic reeks
nautical no longer equipment but a spelling exercise absent of bloom
welfare with its systems-caring
importation with its exporting extirpation
a place to call one's own

PITHING LIKE IMPERTINENT RASH

exfoliate rain   caucus
alchemical kneading
instability volumes cantilever circulation respiration crutch
trafficking in tremolos

TRAFFIC LIKE SAUNTERING DOUGH

accumulation   offerings gift congealing intimacy flares
committee by armorall by verizon by npr by gps by classic rock by ....
conjecture an overworked theme molt dilapidatory in quagmire
inch a hunch away neural transmitters stumble surplus signage
coolants   axle   oil change
jeopardy & falderal
transportation is the opportunity to community
destination heroics   the privilege
of having a place to go
appointed times engineered to feint telos
perpetuation
the fumes
surround sound

WAITER LIKE MIRACULOUS QUILT

the occipital satin the roam pursed
platters slashing with live sinew
the virtuosity of chew
the coronation
the feast sumptuosity the keening
liveliness
of appetite

THE ROAD TO _____ ROAD

THE ROAD TO COMB ROAD

blow dry   green   GPS
triangulation ://: titular
rustlers comb the territory rouse the idlers
the whittle abbreviates then establishes
pursuit   punctuality   paraphrase
profit   predictability
bottom line

THE ROAD TO INITIATION ROAD

spool
underway   undertow   underMonk[9]
umber
halters drip creosote (hitch-up arrears
with winnow
the abbreviate leers
overstake & studded
posthaste the brunt
To Hinge necessitates HALT. A br(e)aking for extreme curves, unexpected
inclines, forbidding terrain.
giddy-up the spur in the saddle
to ride
to partake   brook
all directions
recapture the fumble

---

[9]   smellspellof

THE ROAD TO JOY ROAD

song
    emerald cobbled
th(o)rough way

blister patches irrigated with
novelty rinse ://: lace penumbra
the pan migratory aeolian
colossi
specifying

THE ROAD TO LONELY ROAD

sunkfull, ...   slinkery capsize
bloat   cacophonous caulking
     callow co-ordinates   *(going down)*
reiterant reissues
the calumny that closes a hold a
perfidy a puncture
a skull manufactured
overseas
a pit(i)fa(ult)ll(ful)

THE ROAD TO LOVE ROAD

amorous-*ness*   flowers   promises
love is largely imagining futures together
plans, purchases
.....
turbulence & foul
weather gear
a conundrum a clue a choker a
child
a constellation courting
concinnities

THE ROAD TO NECESSARY ROAD

recombinant   logarhythmic
logging ... perturbative
   perturb as lead-to → stir, stirring
    (arch Soutine   excoriate exhale
       advance
the visceral imperative   further ance
furtherance foreswear adhere repair beware stare appear career freer tear smear
         compulsory forward
     arriving at/coming to   [proceed process procession
reluctance overthreshed mandatory palaver mean streets meander pleat   /cleat
going down the road feeling necessary
routing/root
pursuit a congruence,   a gathering
a womb along   bringing to/ bringing forth
           (coltshooves
the isolate gathers no
the necessary road the
th(o)rough way

WITH

WITH

ACCIDENT, ... delays
pile-ups, ..—claims,
aforementioned erroneous accelerative overflunk
....
eidetic swans in dissimulation
a core autopsy plucking irreverences
an agricultural pathos forsook of belomancy
peppering the overleaf an aphasic statistics
riddles *like*-lihood
'liking,' a curious link to accident
liking = accidental?
cramped in the back seat of reticence
occlusal congregations inspire offspring as replenishment instruments
justification pop-ups
the rallies are hardening
despairing for the road to holy road
a banquet of steer
steer-crazy
dislocative reticulations

WITH

AMMUNITION, ... loaded
packed   „   alerted
on alert   state of
prepared   preparation to
empty into ...
          to defend or attack
               ignitable
....
the entreaty is to
treating the treaty   tread
               thread
bread

WITH

APTITUDE, ...   proclivity
purse   predilection   purpose
ful   fulfilling purpose   destiny flag
flagellant
force ://: obeisance
gifted with ... gifts
giving gifts   bringing into
showering
release
cleanse

WITH

BRAND, ... identity
legitimacy → object-ification, ... ownership
rehearsals
    "I got my brand on you
   There ain't nothin' you can do honey
    I got my brand on you"
settlement-flux
a gravity earned
reins
reign

WITH

BREVITY, ...   brief
elisions   parting to
              pertaining by
the divide   the perforce amputational
to obliterate   approach
to circumscribe   deflate
surfacing the economical
squeezing the apertures
closed

WITH

CASTING , ... embrace,
to tender   tenderize   absorption urge
      thematic throw   color-
ation
last the cast
            make fast
vaporous columnizing
float
devour

WITH

CLUMSY,...   aptitude
on holiday   inepti-tudinous
     coalitional crack
numerical tumble
      jumbling synaptic hierarchical blunder farce
cranky machinery
misfire
   backfire
     transpire
       perspire
delinquency clause

WITH

COMBING SILENCE, ... élan
strains of lore, forecast
hazardous material
the aprons unwinding
lassitudinous laddering
leaning in

WITH

HERD, ... splendor
the more   buildup   mass
                massificence
bunch-bunching   a gather   together
                gathering together
pull pulling   pulling together
                pool-ing
proof   proof reading   reading the herd
        collectivity equations
gyrational carp crowding tissue
                    denizens
labor

WITH

INITIATION,...   root
root matter – Chauvet   Combarelles
Lascaux
image crackles jaws the lot leopards
innards tangle strophe
transition
spool
a bridge   turn   passing   a passageway
passenger
routings   routes   **routing the**
image: port   :tooth-echo   :vessel   :tribal transport   :lead-to
accustomization   thruway(s)
resolution   *ing*
trajectivity numeralized
disorders
settlements

WITH

JOINTURE, ... enterprise
chute   compound
compoundment   mention
ing
feasibility   conjunction
posturing the awry as amateurish scold
a posted blemish a taunt funereal
dismissal
grappling the overture
orchestrating initiation
the pull to
through

WITH

MARRIAGE, ...   vows
continuity contiguity commitment
orientation & orienteering
spilling over & into the cup carrieth
announcing **Other**

the road absentees decorates with
corvine abandonment with the stuff of sandwich
a carry-on a carryover cauliflower curtailings October wings
a dumpster a dimpster a canister carrying canary breast can
relegate the outsourcing of soul soul assembled Im-ported contorted
by mass produced low wage earners by rote over happenstance governed by systems
committees gurus & politicos squeezed shrunk debased extorted then transported
home in the clock of the large now ....
auction
the block the sock – if all sock wearers the world over wore the same color everyday
would that be a step toward unification –
start with the feet proceed upward
resuscitate the breast the promissory note distribute universal daily breast sucking
imperative a need releases the trigger happy universal breast coverage aureole oriole
cupola the face of the road
puckering

WITH

MONK, ...   creamery
field crops apace   {anaconda}   management
classes pole dancing & fire drills
ragout toy metal NYC yellow cabs
      rope tricks to *skyscraper* time
          ornery yet udder
the clunk per-Cussive squid shots single malt proprietary hoop dunks loop-coiling
iguana suns on parade
rocking rupestral cleat   rousing Scottish highland grouse
sentimentality zithers
trespassing on extracurriculars   caution ahead
sanctimony
sagacity
singularly scatting scrump-tu-**O**s-*ities* scrim –
succulence
gnarl fidelities
fruct fornicative fricatives
arrive
jive
festival

WITH

NOISELESS SPEECH, ... remark
remarkability   bruise
purfle

event-ment telling
eyelashes flutter
an ocean regarding

WITH

ORCHESTRATION, ...   plenum
assortments, kind-----------------------------------a vagary
established ... ing   quiddity
terms
....
genre flush   taper
tussling muscle mesh shivering alphabeticals
festoon fibrillate
tuning (tightening/loosening)
correspondences
divagate
                    the
concert

WITH

PERSISTENCE,   agglutination
punctuation layers & candelabra, coercion   robust davening
pivot formation clubfoot androgyny
a species recognition system to circumvent migration
       loopholes   vast vacuities voracious veracity
omniveracity
tangle-feet   ankle-louting
woodwork & inherence
autoconvective ventilation = the draughts insects
create when they flap their wings ...

WITH

PITH, ... substance
surrendering sap
a prow
a manifest destiny
a pertinence

W I T H

P R O L O N G A T I O N , ... maneuver

irritability,   —complaint

.....
purloin quiddity loin launch mastication therapies altitudinous gain no gainsay
quibble

grit grainy to robust go

archaeology   the dig   uncovering

perturbation   pertination

present

WITH

RULES SUBSIDING, ... erosion
relieving a surface   fortuitous
paramour
permits
traveling with insinuation
renewal leases from orthodoxy

WITH

S I L E N T   C O M B I N G , ... attendance
the measures whir ...
analogic a creamery a Percival a
plant
commingling & combing
parts of speech

WITH

SPECIES IMPACT , ...   unravels
deregulation   inchoate incubate
inoculate   include inconclusivity
measure for measure-*less*
{the frenzy conflagrational hazardous unearthed unstoppable
broom the sweep can brindle *un*burden

anachronism is a sweep recalled
heave ho! no time for diddly-doo
pocket the rocket
scramble the amble
fumble rumble products for a longer life hit 'enter'
sizing up a sizzler palatable scrum swarm
ignition spites perdition
with initiation the return admissible

WITH

STILLNESS,...   mauve
perspicuity   pause
elbow hammocking
Satie
branch in Winter drift
oaths swollen non-promising

WITH

SUBTRACTING STRANGERS *...   a peeling
appealing to root   tribunate
emotional triage   (or)   amputation—
stumps vibrating absence   twitching for
formulation—
a cut off   annulling chance encounter fructuosity fa(res)irs
(with) skeletonizing more bone
(//) less flesh less flesh
jointure providentiality   enterprise fork wheelbarrow cart rock
divestiture & sock → rank linings
vacuum   to plunge into to pull through
what we bring, what we discard
rudiments   drumming
with the beat

---

*Hinging to "subtracting strangers" given by/found from Joe Giglio.

WITH

SURREPTITION,...   rent
forestalling abnegation while maintaining a
passion for fables in
light of a failing populace
flags besmirched
marches flagging—
pliancy frottages regulation

WITH

THE STRING OF THE VIOLIN CALLING FOR AIR
                              this
intake   catch   callow   curving scimitar
—*Pythagorean scrambler*—   cuirass cuvette cummerbund wind cue cuniculus cut
the curtain call   comeuppance
escape a lark the devilish turn a dandy do opening night
to pitch the pot pinch the purse distraught the plug display the curse ......
recalcitrance romance rehearse desert the pack ... rummage ... rummage,,,
plumage scrimmage spirits skirmish
the ball's in play relish
lay-a-way pay as you float remote a boat a goat a tote smote the ensemble heigh-ho
alevio
heave from away
we go

WITH

TYSON,... Mike
pulp friction

>speed
>accuracy
>skill
>power
>strength

skullduggery

>legend ://: legacy

options/opportunities

>'knocking everybody out in spectacular fashion'
>'refuse to lose'
>'one objective – win'

>>*(man is a must)*

career/careen/—catastrophe
capital
harvest
gathering force   to accumulate, to muster force/to administer

>'I always try to aim to the back of my opponent's head ... fantasize my
>punch going through'

Cus   Cus the circumscriber   Cus, definitional ... freeing up, providing
framework   the empty canvas   no freedom without limitation
provisioning,—tape up
battlement ://: embitterment   ajar/jarring
personality formation is the struggle for conflicting states/roles/traits to find
settlement (appeasement)
role battling   oppositional traits
identity is our current conception, an accumulation of perceptions bundled into
convenient form, or bundled into form for convenience, an aggregate—does a
shape, a predilection, a talent, emerge, as champion, at the expense of other
impulses, fortitudes, ... does one risk sabotage by one's lesser talents—
role against role, self image against self image, battling for a knockout, for a
Decisive, win,

>*the monolith monster mania // aeration   chiasmus elope*
>*poignance/points*

that god in the ring, the self struggling to formulate, to maintain its formulation,
        careen caretaker cauldron calibrate, boil: steam – stones murking,
        mud lumberers – preciosity seals – the temperature of stone
mental health is talent cultivation is
uppercutting depletives
training is
bringing fore

WITH

UNENCUMBERED, ...   mount
motile   lessening   moist
take away---------------------gain   viri
descence   encouraging swordplay
roustabout   delinquent rain
enigma robes
tantalizing

WITH

WINNOWING , ...   partials, planes
topsy turvy   tuckery
          , (trick
parse parsnip purse perambulate
prickly persnickety positron perspicacity plus
positions nonplus
redeemability incline separatism chief
harvest forecast
metronome calligraphy
qualify cornflower chlorophyll cornucopia, cullclutterclumpcut
cutout
conflagration of parts
discernment
in matters of faith
believability lacks transparency

WITH

WITHSTANDING, ... notwithstanding   with
stand   with can pan fan also ran
resistance
                (smear
persistence consisten
cy confabulation correlation congratulation contrarily inflationary doo wop buzz
insect life   anathema wrings
purchasing predatory counters specializing in wholesale &
u-s-e-d
10 Proven Ways To Flatten Your Stomach
sign-ups   lists   facebookfaceliftfaceUp
futile fibrillatives
futile
the discus
futile discussion withstanding
notwithstanding

WITH _____ THIS _____

WITH BLADE THIS INTO

slice   pierce   slash   in
to   in-to   into {intointointointo}   int(uition)o   pen
e   trat(ion)e   incis(or)e   cist   cistern
  :: a river cuts through ::
  :: throat—a passage ::
  —cutthroat –
  —cutup –
  —cutlery –

—carving a figure— —figure painting—

open   opening   cut open   opening an
entrance-*way*   the *way* int-to   to-ward

the blade vocalizes entrance
appears before
cuts both ways

delivers – edge as departure, incipience – the arch requisite – essential sustenance
– blade → the primal throne

gateway
to
entrance   entranceway
not way-ward   but a
way-to →   *to-ward*
the way to way   the thru-way

the way of the to is the way of the thru
thru the to is the way
the way in the way to   weigh-in   weighing-in
the thru of the way is the to way
the in of the to is the to of the in
the thru of the to is the way of the in is the thru of the in is the way of the to

in-side slide
insideslide   slide in   slideinside
                    —tide tidings

way leads on to way
the road to necessary road

alabaster stalks the sundial blockage a gurgle slap

remote the untouched

blade
the residence

omnibus, ...   ombudsman
respiration extension lung → thrush
thresh
manufacturing
quick apt aptitude
the health about wielding as much as the
welding
tribulations & justice
the court systems
Christ!
what a waste of time

WITH

CRASS LOBOTOMY SCRATCH THIS FOOTAGE

persiflage precipitous persecute perilous no purr chary windup purse
    , clang
the length of demonstrative distance
to slumber slender then climb a number to put you there
to get you there the get is as good as a got the put
you get is the give you got if you good
from novelty this slant the incline
an early stage recognition system a
sli(ght)de to insight to deterministic wayfaring a way to pay if you play your way
sliding into
revelation convenience conveyance convex convexity the knowing
bells like this arguably the shortest route
& why meander when
much proposals butt so rake
at stake

stall ...
    leap leaptdown override pallor parlour frown clown
minstrel without strings no sings
signage across the livery the spoon walks off the table tablespoon teaspoon tea-
spoonful spoonful of tea tea spoons the table enough of these pleasantries the
bread is stale!, Max,
cumbersome crux crudités relax the bid the boast is postmortem
        (night paying for an hour of lapdancing was ground grievously
no lust to wander the staying put   the wonder to wander is wonderful
wanding wonderful is wonderful
warlords permit no growth
afternoons spent delousing warrants

mermaid ↔ alligator   reconnoiter
                              loiter
coital quarter
                        quoit

texture mesh rough ready burly prep plush pearl purling purloin
coping prana
pump inquisitive strain
          flubadubdub
flummox   flummery   disparate   dispute repute
reputations (at stake)   stokery strike
tales toss tough fusing millennial musing
                              telluric tickle
bumps   protuberance   integument
belly slippery slink jawing horizon-ship ://: sea horse breastr(w)ise angularity
          angling ang(und)ulations   gildering calyx

                        [border posses
                        foreign affairs
fireside chats
a species trapeze   interdiction trapdoor   the
commingling imperative   kin in *tailspin*   splash shimmering incandescent
glitter coils
                  breezing to
juxta-posit-IOning
                              {cocktail hour
                              shall we dance
                              getting to know you
                              if loving you is wrong, I don't want to be right
mermaid bobbing benzedrine bait
shorelines
lapping

ability to employ   usage
usage factor   bring around   (come around
coming around   becoming sound
serving sound   becoming sound-*ness*
weeping as contrivance   as conveyance factor
ordering, placing, —placement
emit emission
conveying → breakout
weeping
dislodge
hectoring forward

SMELLING

SMELLING CONTRITION

lime based
magnolia   peach tree ... forlorn
the overcast repudiates the harelip mastering
the western scale necessitates practice
ankle bells the walls dance
21 seasonal volleys
before the tumble

SMELLING LOVE

onion [*no*] ... oleander, gardenia
[*better*] .... cusp crepuscular
trampoline emerald emanations crush
perpendicular [*jam on*]
mule mud   turpentine trust deposits
ammonia swells   café cankers
      bluff barnacles basement cleat [*yeah*]
crull angels pitching spaciousness
between the lines

SMELLING PRESSURE

            pressur   i
zation   iza   tion
        steam   roll
steam roller   gathering   (herd?
   (herd like?   confluence (congruence?
against   build-up   buil-ding   (flock
blow your lid   don't blow your lid   keep your cool
resistance
keep your lid on
.....
l e t

MODULAR MODIFICATION

With this Hinge Event the particle is *not* submitted to differing modular constructions for voluminization, but, rather, is unfolding as the result of modifying a pre-existing modular condition. The Module mutates as it matures. A ripe, mature organism is primed to interact vitally with its environment. When the organism/environmental relationship achieves a certain level of "settlement" (stability), robust organisms will seek to expand their frontiers. Mutation/Modification enables the efficacy of those extensions. The modifiers (mutations) emerging in *fstr* are "were there," and "if." They are included in this volume as "indicators"; — to indicate fertile areas that this practitioner has not had the time to fully develop and which might encourage others to pursue.

Modular Modifier – "were there"

WERE THERE CHATTER LIKE BANALITY FLUSH

sewage   crapola   wasteland weighing upon
wasteland   cyber-promiscuities   perpetual redundancies
percussive trivia clamors
what would the Rilkean Angel?
what would Ecstaticus?
strategies:
furl in mad twistings fern the gadget-e-torial cemeteries fan perspicuities with
quixoticisms discount the countable
saddle idle meditations the unmanned the unforeseen, ... thought-full-ness
fill thought   full-thought   thoughtfillingfull-fills
careen barter foster cupcake chocolate fawn dispensers
levitate
altitudes

deliberations, ...   conferences
focus groups
                (PA Systems
would there develop a Hunger Strike
a collective "NO" –
what would: proprietorship
              proprietor
              diversions
              jobs   ?
what bailout plans
what proposals
slaughters or liberations

if no docility, what historical revisionism – no chariots, no cavalry, no fear raising
Mongols – warfare redefined

absenting horse from barn, from domesticating possibilities, would horse, deprived
of human concert be extinct today? how would this horse absenteeism impinge the
human landscape? how we've been accoutered by horse – archetypically,
imagistically, artistically, agriculturally, ... hunting, herding, roping, cowboying, ...
leisure activities, sports, races, show, dressage, hunter-jumper, ... the merry-go-
round ... –
horse outcropping the human festival

if no horse would/could there be a substitute
what would the substitute look like
zebras don't domesticate well

> Today wolves,
> panthers, and
> elephants vanish, ..
> dogs, cats, and horses
> flourish.

did the horse choose us? co-opt us? humanity as their gravy train?
almost unthinkable to think that we could extract horse from our mental
environment
imagine the thought of no horse   deleting every horse image that scrambles to
mind
empty of horse
horse-*less*

WERE THERE MERMAID LIKE RECALCITRANT THRUSH

→ →→→ ebullition, ...   prosperity banks
solar saddles spelunking pampas remorse apposition apotheosizing bass clarinets
apothecarial sequester harpsichordal scream
       no feet for religions to rely upon
       the graphic build-up shutters
       wind a congregational power
       the Pharisees grow furtive
       the lessons withdraw
       haberdashery clusterwraps caulk the sidewalk

the brew
specializing in provincial calyces

judgment day   the boot heels cakey
an appearance wreaked, flappable .... unhealthy
unhealthy with odor & malfeasance
with bearing barely pluckery no fin
assembly/dissolution—& shot through that
process – assembling/disassembling – cancellation
craters, obviation cancers, dismemberment agents –
there is neither becoming nor
unbecoming, but perpetual
semblance
a version of
unruly

Modular Modifier – "if"

IF FROM MERMAID THIS TAIL

proposal, ...   proposition
illustration

the text is awash with celerity
spermatozoa uncertain, ... ferocious

the suggestivity of proposition
as if it were a color burning
raspberry on fire
its ashes fawning
swishing seductions & follow-ups   a
fable dismounting
a tribe
unwinding

IF IN THE TEMPERATURE OF BARN

a sigil
a feather
a warlord
v(b)anished joinery rejoining

temperature bathing effluvial larynx
boughs secreting fraternity blossoms
                laryngeal phalanx
travel aids latch to odes streaming the old beams
memory shuttles through nostril's windpipe

nostrums concocted evaluated culled
will medicinals ever serve for the notching
are there spare parts in the hoof
reins of guidance

FUSION RECONNOITER

employs two disparate modules bearing the identical particle and fuses them into a new creation. To preserve reproductive integrity, each element in the individual modules must appear in the birthing.

: Individual Application :

JOURNEY LIKE AUTOCHTHONOUS TRYST

wayfarers   space faring dispositions
  —land sea air— merchants
of getting there
t(h)read
     the way found is the way lost
     the road to lost road
revolutions bursts procedures
mechanisms to displace
departure arrival to arrive at the point of departure is a departure
there
from to
here
travel is a meditation upon where
whereabouts
you are are: a conceptual congress
a beacon hopping duck bills saddle sores flat feet lower lumbar
getting closer a compromise
the best
we can do

THE ROAD TO LOST ROAD

epoxy garlic   the restraints
uneasy no longer fabric   sustenant
billow   a cut in the canopy
the passing lane squirting mongoose
churlish with zoology the engines spit
metering begins with equipment
          , a rough trade
vehicular inspections on a regular basis augment counterfeit
identity speeds
the chord finds its way

: FUSION :

journey like autochthonous tryst
    reconnoiters
        the road to **lost** road

wayfarers   epoxy garlic
   sustenant billow   space faring disposition
the restraints uneasy no longer fabric — land   sea   air — merchants of canopy
a cut in the passing lane squirts mongoose spit
churlish with zoology the road to lost road engines
a rough trade   the metering begins
with equipment revolutions bursts procedures   t(h)read vehicular inspections
on
a regular basis   the way found is the way lost
the chord finds its way
departure arrival to arrive at the point of departure   is a departure
mechanisms to displace whereabouts
there   from
here
to
travel is a meditation upon where
identity speeds
are: a conceptual congress
are you a beacon hopping duck bills saddle sores flat feet lower lumbar
a compromise
getting closer
the best we can do

: Individual Application :

SONIC LIKE ALTITUDINOUS SKIN

ramparts smithereened   glabrous glow
         earthenware
skein & the development of nomenclature
agricultural imperatives

sickles grazing upon glaziery
breathing on naked geometries

: Individual Application :

IN THE SONIC OF STONE

a mercy land   merriment displacements
gatherings that regroup from upheavaling
unearthly glances   eyes, lifetimes to decipher

trombones skipping across the sea
a form of prayer

: FUSION :

sonic like altitudinous skin
        reconnoiters
           in the sonic of **stone**

naked geometries sickle glaziery
              breathe upon
trombones skipping across merriment displacements
                    smithering earthenware
regroup rampart gatherings from upheaveling the sea

eyes dazzle to decipher lifetime glances glabrous glow
                        grazing on a mercy land

agriculture & the skein of development unearth
prayer
forms of imperative a nomenclature

FECUNDATING ROTATIONAL CLUSTER

is paradigmatic of Particle Densification. From this rotational kinetic, we witness "stone," "plangency," and "sonic," volumizing through multiple modular submissions. As they outcrop from shifting perspectives – fold-ins ://: flood-outs – the impregnated particles become Mass-Emboldened, Stature Enriched. —*Molten larval modules burbling on the ground of being.*

It is the destiny of every application to participate in FRCs. Another way of saying this, is that each application is *Cluster-Bound.*

[Is the being of Being being Out-Sourced?]

The Fecundating Stone Rotational Cluster

FROM STONE THIS RUNNING

ambidexterity   ambergris
    alightment   lighting
a-lighting   lightning ...
strickening aperture urge emerge
activity mounts   mountains
of quizzicals
the purge to cross
cross-over
turns
returns

FROM RUNNING THIS STONE

adroit   skidstop   turn
  roundabout   periscope up
             , decency
             , docent
pocket press(ing)ure
well-managed congestion
a chamber adroit—
               sultry sonata sinecure lull
aquarium filled encomium farm
ripe

FROM STORM THIS STONE

outriggery   caulk caul cauldron
coiling   coin   encoiling   encoding
                        clusterclub
perturbative prolix ailing caterwaul crinoline curling collapse syndrome

vortex   pretext   asunder
splits
rupture
revel
ation

FROM STONE THIS TEMPERATURE

this ↓→ time of day
    situationism

to curtsy glance cumulous comeuppance   a
stance   beckonings & features
vertebrae clavichord blinking hymnal streams
beseechment dice delirial traffic, rock
with Monk this stone rising to an overmastering quiescence
glee curtains
             pillow lacings
slippering

FROM ISSUE THIS STONE

embed   embedding   recalcitrant
                    yet
in the throat of stone this lair
vocal stretch   campaign oblong
an heredity matched by combustion & necromancy
a darling of mosaic
                    , lachrymae rich
sound
foggery

IN THE STONE OF SONIC

timbre   timpani   tremolo
                     (petulance
petulance bedded   bedecked   bedizened
a vehemence troweling tonal rills
creation ://: eruption
abatement ladders
terminal velocities
a vacuum of
blottings

IN THE TEMPERATURE OF STONE

dank   drool cool   dark   drapery maroon   indigo blue
parsnips   a wind
burly
curly
barely a wind at all
a broken breeze
              simoom swan
wind crutching
              guarding
providence
              gradations
steps & ladders
a sofa chair

IN THE THROAT OF STONE

measurement then device
alternatives like contraband weighing
perturbative rinse

the shallows in cloak
dams restored
handicraft

IN THE VERTEBRAE OF STONE

cartilaginous quizzicals
                           [vertebra, from *vertare,* to turn.
correspondences   aid assembly
the marching band
                         upon which
stacked convolutes
                                giving rise to
                                girding
                                griding
gridlock
       grind
           grandstand

interstitial
space makes music
                     {aria
                     {redemption
bend   arch   wiggle
      twist
the palace of claim grows
curates

STONE LIKE ANFRACTUOUS LUST

gather   gathering   in   a place to gather
                       housing
in being enlarging (be)(become) becoming being   enlarging enlarges being
                 enlarging becomes being
   —serpentine tortuous twist template tantrums
—perfidious frocks
robustly rollicking   **Rock**
swirls seismic swarm   , storm
voluptuosity brewing
carapace   casing
washing
away

THE ROAD TO STONE ROAD

step   stepping   stepping stones
                                steep
                                a log up
stone is not sludge is bone
                        is ledge-worthy
crepuscular with quiver
                    {stone *dancer*
                    {rock *shaker*
rubberizing lawn moan
                    complete pleat   replete
omnivorous can be(come) an acquired taste
gorging on rainbow
                end of
street of screams   only a dream away
fulfilling the stone
stone zone
the road
the path

The Fecundating Plangency Rotational Cluster

IN THE ESSAY OF PLANGENT

maroon, ...　　moor moored
　　　{mournful}
alabaster clunkage
parlance oversized, ... ruddy
wastelands seething with pit practice arch proclivities locus perambulatories
blanch

equinoctial sophistries
conventions compromised
loot matter governs the infidels
peals
in the sack of curl

IN THE ASSAY OF PLANGENCE

avowal   attestation   arousal
plangere ...

locomotive
lumber
sickling lubricity counters
counterweights   signage   /ambassadorials

ambrosial
pining
cottoning plunge

PLANGENT LIKE ACRIMONIOUS THIRST

tubular trump   voiding vernacular
catarrhal sulk
grievance ↔ contrivance
cell free zone
acknowledgments: information source
descry (desecrate)
huckleberries
purifying water
toward untoward
untoward

PLANGENT LIKE INGLORIOUS HOST

catarrhal   caterwaul   wreak
eke cutouts   cutthroat exempt
expedition expire expir-ing
          piracy in treble clef
thirsts non-hoistable   quench warfare
funereal undersides absence
          societal catacombs
civility shuckshorn skirmish surrept crept crepitate catatonia Catalonia   caribou
cunt
celestial incompetence, blear
bleat
glut factories
considerations
tear/tear
tearfully

SMELLING PLANGENT THIS ARREST

clump arrears covenant   illogical sap suppling
the diocese
caught in the middle a mummery a mock-up a merman meridian meddling a
muddle modifiable protests identifiable smirked over
clandestine
quirks quarks quarantine
lipswelling
swollen
contraband

IN THE PLANGENT OF STONE

plaint   batterings logy with
lachrymose   bleat
patterings
a judgment call
cataract preempt
streaming water therapies light
embellish the wash
considerations

The Fecundating Sonic Rotational Cluster

FROM SONIC THIS EQUIPOISE

                  (after Tannery Brook

catchall   collaboration   cutthroat
                            (poise
                          critical
leathery rendering   sound of wear
             wear sounding
suppling cohabitational particle collusions sprint enharmonic scaling feints
accomplice ensiform scumbling sluice cataract campfire roundabout marshmallow
petitionings
                         slurs
                    slice
                            slips
                               scull
               ing
scythe rumble scalp promissory m(pl)oan
                  plaint
(pliant (compliant
flame flounce flamingo petticoats s(au)(or)cer(y)(ie)s spinning
                           (spun conjugationals

              pla
        int
           ive
                  ly
tumbling
encomium
             dispositional grace
ecclesiastic spur   larkspur
      hark the heralds
mark spark   re-mark   rivuletr(t)inglingaleviobringing
combing dash interval allegiance hatchings saunter sarabande
sinewy tendon sargasso strategies shuffle

water/rock/lap
    era(compo)sure
establishing   pouring insessorial
tributes
          trib
    u
       taries
         arials
               crewel calibrates
       lodgings ://: dislodgings
sickl*ing*
     spring-*ing*
sing – *in*
g

IN THE STONE OF SONIC

timbre   timpani tremolo
                      (petulance
petulance bedded   bedecked   bedizened
a vehemence troweling tonal rills
creation ://: eruption
abatement ladders
terminal velocities
a vacuum of
blottings

IN THE STORM OF SONIC

troubadourian juvenilia   outposts/
intrigue   bestiality swathes, turret
compromises   relief forms in jeopardy
hypnogogia no longer permissible
pitted borings fitful relentless rapscallion
Etna is no longer the high parishioner but irresponsible
scarcity entrances a scarcity exercise
entrancement

the mufflings we've
abandoned

SONIC LIKE (S)WELTERING CARP

swill rings   capstones   gowns of
blue whistle   comfort bottle   apertures
slight yet omnipresent
sonic a bend a blend
        a plot
        a got
koi flush cocktail blaze plush remonstrance
pursuant to liquidity fluidity
Debussy's *Suite bergamasque* trespasses barefoot upon overworked diplomas
hatchet warriors unline their faces, grow sultry, pedal rhinestones for flair
color a catch in an eighth note jeopardy
a parade of ambiguities mobilized by harem spittle
banner an explanatory prestige

WITH SONIC THIS TESTUDINEOUS LULLABY

poised   plum
                      plumb line
equipoise   testudo blanket irenic wrap
secure sure soothe-couth   youth protect
har(la)boring young   snug songs
surrogate warmth
sinkfulls
pointed instruments
 pointedly

THE INTERFECUNDATING ROTATIONAL CLUSTER COLLUSIONAL

(re)presents the inter(breeding)activity between two or more FRCs upon coll(usion)ision. The term "collusion" is employed here to evoke how strictly the "Truthful" veers from the Institutional.

The Interfecundating Trespass/Query Rotation Cluster Collusionals (see below) outcrops this newly appearing Hinge Behaviorism.

* Appearing for the first time is a modular development I am terming "The New Theater." It introduces conceptual dialogue into the Fecundating Rotational Lingua-scape. As a primarily discursive modality, it dramatically enables particle voluminization. The concepts are the characters. "Border broaching Trespass" represents "The New Theater."

The Interfecundating Trespass/Query Rotation Cluster Collusionals

TRESPASS IN OBDURATE CREDULITY

purloin   partition
caul   caterwaul   cakewalk
     — *caulk* —
saw-scat triplet jabberwocky plasticity is a form of persuasion submariners gauge oxygen deliberate horological witchcraft   craft often misconceived as attendance bears scrutiny normally sanctioned by parsimony   the veto carries the format undertow shimmy *grab a hold in desperate ways* the planks are tumbling

VENTURE WOUND

peelings   layer-scrapes
     lungfulls

                  t

          o

        r

integumental rip
         plunge to deep bedding

                      to

the ruin that collapses
        (de-lic-ious-ly

obliterating
vesicular clot
ventricular absenteeism
mute colors eloping to the hides of albino crocodile

all is let
wound bled unto wound
pools of blood theme
upcharges amplitudinously de-curtaining
throbbing

spooling thrones of immaculate enquiry

TRESPASS LIKE LOLLING LIQUIDITY

undercurrents
                    locks-void
  exposure
    expose
      exposition
wound
        wound-ing

wind
winding
venturing wound windings *comb -*

        - ing

[[**trespass ventures the wound**]]

the breakdown effloresces gratuitously & with dispatch

sea urchins squealing for signature the uprisings more frequent   more fervid

pastries laden with grumblings greater than commotion command the outposts,
the earthenware creaks

how to judge a trajectory void of destination

dispositions dissimilarly aroused spell odd contractions

the leftovers no longer consumable

TRESPASS IN CUMULATIVE BRUISE

chomp   chaw rust gardens
barbed wracking skin
raking paw
batter flounces
comeuppances come quizzical with lamentation distillate with wet
wolves come with eyes
the fang in the hind
mobility

BORDER BROACHING TRESPASS

B: Why?

T: Why what?

B: What makes you do it? Why take the risk?

T: It makes me tingle. Makes me feel alive.

B: And if you get caught?

T: I'm caught uncatching.

WITH

TRESPASS, ... divagate
deviate
delinquency ...
.....
delve
de-liv-
erance

WITH

LAMENTATION, ...   dusk
dearth   dirigible   dirge
straits preamble out of step corn-swollen conditional

swollen   →   sinkage
coming-over   over-coming
bridge the interloper
groundswell
anchoring cohabitation in forms of dice

IN WANDERING THIS LUST

grippage   tracting   a tail a quirk a
sputterance   feathering utterance throes
jangly juncture posses positioning puncture drills
aboriginal & holding

lamentation lollipop moan   snelling cornerstone fragrance modules
the stone low in its shadow
showers overcast
vigilance
bruising

QUERYING IN PULSATIVE TRUNK

emperors did it puissantly
     forumlative ://: disintegrative
avenging ://: senescent   prior
to the maturation of repudiation
when zoning was honest & the
councils were aboveboard the
galleys wet unkempt grunge latrining
men's minds interlocutors fumble resolution the causeway to
unclog whinny when all was clearly
zero pursuing reduction
    tremulous   perfervid
unwieldy
the
algae

QUERY LIKE COLLAPSIBLE FRUIT

meltdown   bunchings
      seed
serrying nonplussed pagodas pulsative trunk options expire timelines skewer
consideration mycelium directional monastically alert

seedfall   collapse enabling abandon
      abandon creating collapse
dissolution merriment

Query weds Trespass

Q: I can't live without you.

T: You always know what to say.

Q: What is the root of saying?

T: Forage.

QUERY IN DELIBERATIVE DOMAIN

speculation trumped the roundup flareful ardour pump
press evidentiary

        triste elopement

tertiary meld blend the velocities produce a sustainable sleep for stone
an undulant sea for piracy

what wild animal can canker the eye

IN THE SLEEP OF STONE

bedding   pause
pause drowse dripping
pacing dromedaries
silicates
looting the louche galleries

lurk dare
burn / intercourse(s) / interstitials
analogous service stations fulfilling

the caliber of tones inebriate with congregation

QUIZZICAL WITH LAMENTATION DISTILLATE WITH WET

burrowing probe:

Query, in its disposition to forage integrally, weds trespass for profitable sinkage

Sinkage: the veer bypassing appearance

Lamentation: the dirge of trespass wailing to excel the appearing

Kiki Rheeet Rheeet, … Rheeet Kiki!
diabalo doppelganger dungeon-dagger
Rheeet!

alumni reapproved by council congress for orderly matters

elderly are alderly

otherly plum suckle crimson rose

along the sickle steam sliding the wildly restless perturbative adopts evaluation as a
mannerism   — tremors along the wrist
          — worry lines in the canvas

the prayer meetin' says it won't be long

HINGE TABULATORIES

The employment of Mathematical Devices to Interbreed with the Linguistic Components. So, — **Interbreeding Mathematical Devices (IMDs).** Along the lines of a Mathematical/Linguistic Hybridization, i.e. utilizing mathematics to alter the value of the particle, the word.

TABULATORIES

alacrity2 + alembic2 =
enhanced predisposition
ality
remarka bility   formulaic fructosity

alacrity x alembic =
magical squid

alacrity – alembic =
foreshortening

alembic – alacrity =
deprivation,
                ... amputational

alacrity/alembic =
                ... questionable

PLACEMENT

denotes those applications that activate with-in settlement (settle-ins) rather than from pivot/spring-off. Generally it seems to apply to subject matter where much material has already aggregated, thus requiring a differing *attention-set* than explorations denuded of pile-up. An analogy might be the performance of a tracking dog hotly pursuing a scent, rapidly assimilating information as it charges forth, only to stumble upon a scent requiring slow-down, // prolongation //, a curious scent that breaks/interrupts the steady onward, that necessitates pause, circling, consideration and process, a crucial gathering preparative to streaming forth. Placements may be arrived at via the module(s) and most certainly will embed and shootoff modules. Modules that are embedded in the placement we term **EEDs – Embedded Explosive Devices.** An example of an EED would be "the road to more road," which is in the "Slam Incunabula" section of the placement Excoriate Exhale.

It is now known that Placements are also powerful **Application Magnets.** In the same manner as they are fertile domain for the development of Modules & Applications, they also serve to attract already rendered applications, latching on/coupling to insight sources that have been previously magnified. The Hinge Universe at this time is now rooted in the 4 p's: the pivot, the particle, the postulate, and the placement.

CYMBALOLOGY

Zildjean   Sabian   Meinl   Wuhan
metallurgical crash cousins synoptic palimony   circumlocu-navihabitational
thinnest of instruments   sound
resounding bound round   clown sound
pound down clown round   pound pound ping a-ling
Samba sound Rock Mambo Hop Night In Tunisia sound
go round round around bound   circu-larity   cymbal-solidarity
cymbal-hilarity cymbal celerity
cymbal-sizzle cymbal pop cymbal singularity
singularly cordial-convivi-*al*-ity

[This is an installation piece. The Galaxy Gallery in Chelsea created an acoustical marvel to showcase my CymbalOlogy installation. Cymbals from around the world, cymbals of all shapes and sizes, are arranged in Smash-Fashion. Striking implements—sticks and mallets, brushes, etc.—are placed on wall mounts to enable gallery guests to contact the various cymbal-essences. The Galaxy Gallery champions the world's first Cymbal-Scape.]

:: The cymbal was first used by an orchestra in the 1680 opera *Esther,* by Nicholas Strungk, performed in Hamburg, Germany. The Zildjean company in the United States manufactures the most widely used cymbals in the world. The company has been making cymbals by a secret method since 1623. ::

A musical cymbal sound is one that blooms or grows after it is set in motion.
amalgamation agglomerator cruise missiling diameter stretches a shame if
Kangaroos lose that grace
identifying marks establish creature-*hood*   the bell is cymbal-hood
          (*salt solutions salinity palpable saliva stations*)
providential-ity   in psalm 150, David exhorts "Praise him upon the loud cymbals;
praise him upon the sounding cymbals." and here they come, the janissaries, loud
sounding and Terraplane rousing, with their armies, their shouts and hurrahs, their
edged weapons spitting fire, their clanky shields whacking through enemy and
field, surmounting fiefdom and moat, sound as support as chronicler and bastion
basher as cavalry and charger siege engines trebuchet trench counterweight torsion
master masterful mankind mastermind cymbal STRike
cymbal MiGHT

the sound of two great cities – New York & London, or Paris, say – performing, ris-
ing up, melted and hammered into format, tempered, and should they strike in this
fashion, crash together, two giant Cymbal-Cities (New York & London, or Paris,
say), & were it pleasing, would other cities conjoin, succubussed by the music in
their ears, their very marrow ringing, could this be the start of a movement –
Barcelona & Naples—*********
Chicago & Baghdad—*********
Tampa & Tehran—*************
Moscow & Mogadishu—*********
Milano & Michigan—*************
Bogotá & Berlin—***************
Sao Paulo & Reykjavik—####********
will this sound production, ringing from the center to the extremities, create a
global giddiness, a planetary parade – drum sticks, bass drums, cymbal crashes,
trumpet voluntaries, color garrisons overloaded, unconventional and ultra-beam-
ing, could this musicality/communality/commonality (and why not) produce a
paradigm shift, a political revolution, a … – **P-A-R-T-Y!!?**

and does this (and why not) spell an invitation to the solar system to respond,
to behave in kind, for earth to clay & clang with Moon and then with Venus, &
Venus with Mars, & Mars with Jupiter, inciting a chain – planetary – reaction,—
each planet being granted a "musical-leave-of-orbit," & as this jangling carillon
honking prospers, producing squeals & peals of planetary ploans, won't other
galaxies take notice, desire to plunge into this alloy spinning dervish fest, …

Important to the symphony orchestra is contrast. Seek exaggerated highs & lows in choosing your cymbals. Cymbalic mood swings. Prescription drugs to promote Cymbal-Calm ....

'working the iron cymbals
I take the low road gouges
in the esophagus of the right eye

nuyon kidi
nuyon kadan
nuyon kada
tara dada i i'

corralling the gold cymbals
I load the high road gauges
in the big toe of the engine room

cyber spume   crypto cycadaceous syllogistic jisms
splash sumptuosities
crackling correlative cambiatas

cymbalogy-biology-symbology-astrophysiology
cartographygeographytopographyapostrope

Suggested Cymbal Soundings:
Chico Hamilton's 32 second *Eric's time, Romeo and Juliet,* Mozart's opera *The Abduction from the Seraglio,* Beethoven's *Ninth Symphony,* Max Roach's simoom-cymbals / tongue-wafters/on *Delilah/Clifford Brown & Max Roach,* Elvin's entrance on *A Love Supreme* – buoyed harem sizzle – Rachmaninoff's *Piano Concerto No.2,* the *New World Symphony, Das Rheingold, Sheherazade,* ... your *hometown marching band*

'Most cymbals are made of an alloy comprised of varying percentages of copper, tin, & silver. After the cymbals leave the hammering area, they are lathed for a consistent & uniform taper. Lathing is a process in which the oxidation is removed and tonal grooves are added.'

Schooling/lathing – school children de-oxidized, spun into vapor, vapid mind pits, calcification clusters, wrapped around technical gadgetry, drips spilling—intensive care unit—from their brains,
mind-lathing our young with – unlike cymbals – no redeeming sound feature

'Characteristics that affect timbre are the bell size , cymbal weight & profile. The larger the bell, the more overtones the cymbal produces.'

shoaling buoyancy fanfare dollop truce
a fruit repast   calabash, pineapple, oranges, gourds zingling from cymbal
slake
a flying citrus fiesta   encountering in air, seed spluttering playful humbuggery
         tintinnabulation saltatory salutation stall

B.B. King's *Lucille* truss rod endlessly rocking

'A full sound is one that produces partials. It is not the distinct sounds but rather one broad articulation that blends the sound of both cymbals.'

coming together the coming together & entailment outcome contact outcroppings the misuse the use the downright utility/futility of entity-crash... no abbreviation capable of diagnosing the plagiarisms of horn flagellant overexposed bushwhack cafe air pocketed coffers trilogy

does one morph free like sound? an emotional organism rippling into the ether? at point of contact, where is one? suction cusped? compressed into a dualistic blur? a duality posturing fusion? a flight to the elusive and legendarily promising One?

navigate sound, laboratize sound, navigate contact-ings, penetrations, trip the peel
lids to child slide boatswain bowsprit pistol whip the blueprints
                                        gas firing
oven splutter triadic marshmallow sundae sliver timbre palette roastings
     psychedelic blues biopsies   dream bends   climax seeds
     sequin hammers
glimmer arousal jostlings splash eighteenth century enlightenment rakings

Hal Bennink at Tonic 1/9/07:
'I play what they give me. I used to bring my own cymbals... but now I play what is there. My goal is to come into town with a matchbox and 2 matches and play the hell out of it.'

to the playground
to play is to ground
                    to be ground-*ed*
clown sound resound bound round
            formica filly growth the bloom
frills & flummeries
            frolic frolic candle bake
            show me yours I show you make

rousing mandibular veracity fustigant perse

playground corporeal coil corporal the body preach the body Sound the Body Cymbalic!
lungs collude & collide – oxygen SPlash
kidneys thunderclapping
right atrium/left atrium
small intestine/large intestine forte-piano crash // clams prestidigitating
vulva lips
testicle gong
buttocks bash
hallelujah hip lock hammerheads
traditional hand hammered cymbals in pure B20 bronze
smash lash envelope CRASH

'For I was Inca but not King.'
                    (Elvin cymbal scintillator
and I am stable and horse in the dying heart of the cloud
ringing perpetuosity prayers from fractious plates
palettes unwhettted & scolded *on the eve of levitational storm*

Sources:
    1. *The Ultimate Guide to Cymbals* by Nick Petrella.
    2. Antonin Artaud quotations from *Here Lies* (Exact Change, Boston, 1995, page 201).

HORSE

the digits cobbling
                clubbing the hoof corral
peristalsis
hooves of crepitant
this surge   these leggy prancers   these scrupulous gymnasts throaty upon the
earth
most noble animal
sprig nymph   Godiva shareholder
first lute master
choir of mighty gallopers
sing

rearing peals of skyscrape thrall
the trot that establishes then oozes gallop

Pegasus
Bucephalus
Trigger
Xanthus
Man O' War
Whistlejacket
Hi Yo Silver

harness is a construction for intimacy
strapless intimacies, ... amassments
    Horse is one of the few marvelously muscled , airily coursing animals that doesn't
want to eat you.
to cantilever the stirrup a time of reprieve and renewal
saddle up
giddyup
loosed in the ecumenical corral these nuzzlings:
Xenophon says, in his *The Art of Horsemanship:* "And in his frame, the first things
which I say you ought to look at are his feet."
Eohippus[10] piano-ing the earth, to play upon the earth as if you were tickling your
beating heart beneath it, to spectate that...

the individually segregated congregating to hoof, a clopped ensemble, can support
more mass, now percussive, more of a striking instrument,
fingers, ... fist/club
support is an instance of mass
piggyback the man

Virilio writes: "Man is the passenger of woman, not only at the time of his birth,
but also during their sexual relations.... Paraphrasing Samuel Butler, we could say
that the female is the means that the male found to reproduce himself, that is to
say, to *come* to the world. In this sense, woman is the first means of transportation
for the species, its very first vehicle, the second would be the horse with the enigma
of the coupling of dissimilar bodies fitted out for the migration, the common
voyage."
From this, we seek to explore the phenomenology of man's initial dismount from
his primary vehicle, to mounting his secondary.
dismount... dissolution?
is the desire to mount the horse, this more steeply alterior body, an erotic impulse,
an impulse to exotic. What does the exotic offer? Is each serial vehicle – woman[11],
horse, train, automobile, airplane – an additional erotic encounter?

range of motion explicates
idea hopping – abstraction mounts?
with

mount(ing), ... here
to bring forth   covering
to cover,   on top of ...
climb upon, to *en*-counter   *voicings*
the over and under   attaching
attach-*ments*   the cling to

---

[10] Eohippus or Hyracotherium, the earliest believed ancestor of the horse. "They had four toes on
their front feet and three toes on their hind feet. Each toe ended in a separate small hoof. Large,
tough pads similar to those on a dog's foot kept the toes off the ground. These pads bore the ani-
mal's weight." The text is exploring the ancestral telluric sensitivity prior to the padded toe evolv-
ing into the more hardened hoof.

[11] Woman/man is meant to be used interchangeably with no gender pronouncements – other than
child-bearing – intended.

umbilical soundings   to further
to go
gather
in an ensemble (to assemble)
erasing the self in this act of twinning

romance bridles//strapped intimacies
the support bra
support and port
demiurge   the urge to move is the urge to extinguish where you are
with

wheel, ...   rotation,
go round & round, to
& away from   rubbering to jointure   dis-
misses here delivers there
proximity legislator
campaign manager
reeling cartographer

to mount the horse to mount the machine is to breakthrough the borderline, it is
to trace oneself out of the isolate self, it is a gesture toward Alterior Organization...

"As a species, horses could not have survived without human intervention.
Humans could not have created wealth-generating (and, for that matter, leisure)
opportunities that come with large cities without horses. As the perceptive 1881
New York Times editorial observed, 'Deprived of their human servitors, the horses
would quickly perish; deprived of their equine servitors, the human population in
cities... would soon be in straits of distress.'"[12]

Horse is bridge, is root splurging through sinew, is a sienna siren strophing the cur-
vatures of an outsourcing periphery sonata, is the declamation in foetal bounding,
the orchestral lightning spraying through the forelegs of a rearing defiance...

---

[12]   Clay McShane and Joel A. Tarr, *The Horse In The City: Living Machines in the Nineteenth*
   Century (Baltimore: The John Hopkins University Press, 2007), 178.

"Among the Scythians, when a leader died, his horses were killed & buried with him. The expectation was that they would be re-animated to serve the dead man in the afterlife."

Re-Animation:
stallion black heaves from the stable cuckold-winds toss manefuls kicks & furies prows vertical lavades to erring Jezebels – conveyors of halters grooms stables whips saddles coachmen riding crops all manner of tack rupture annihilative – the landscape grows cumulous sinewy, voluptuous mares trot from the forest, the black glee grows, pony stallions squeeze from his monumental shoulders, the de-humanization is vast & good, it is sound, pools of union flutter the tribe, there is intercourse & pawings...

Consideration:
& horse looked unto man & saw that man was puny & would need speed, elevation, & haulers, saw that they could provide man with horsepower (33,000 foot pounds of work per minute) & great diversion & prove a showpiece & companion & understood that man could be good & could care for horse & would mitigate a great many perils that might befall in the wild & horse considered long & mightily & chose man to groom him & feed him & to tutor him in the dance... & man undertook horse & prospered & to this day no other animal summons the monies that horse does...

Diastema

(A long muzzle allows the horse to keep an eye out for danger while grazing. An evolutionary side effect of the lengthened muzzle is the *diastema,* the gap between the incisors & premolars that makes the placement of a bit possible.)

the cradle of ...
          cradling
civili ...   a correspondence construct
anatomical conduit
articulation opportunity (offering)
rein maker
a pocket privileging
a designation trafficking
the obligatory coefficient

I sit by a window seat at P.J. Bernstein's eating a Reuben sandwich while boys in baseball outfits file by. I don't see them young, & pert, but wizened, limp, wrinkled, ... broken. Their eight year old faces are fifty, sixty, eighty years. They march without youth. With faces they wouldn't recognize.

hoofed animals without horns gearing toward rein
that space
the distance between realizations
a pasture
a frisson
excitable stone

In The Temperature Of Barn

... barley, burlap, briar –
    HORSE

"The places most horses these days are looked after, and loved, and where they learn a great deal about the ways of the world they must live in is – the barn."

the pedagogy of enclosure
the pedigree of limit
back rolling mesas clambering glee coulees wind drunk leg celerity kick scramble
—*stall*—
stalling in stall
that wintry redolence bare-fisted perfervid
does the horse whisperer hear the
scream
the bat barristers proffer a wing advocacy
minerality musk

The Reeking Hour—

the Magyars the Huns the Mongols the Mauritanians the Goths
the Scythians the Apaches the Comanche & the Blackfoot –
the great horse cultures
swinging with the horse, an equestrian bebop, a bandstand eureka
from the planks the floorboards the walls an archetypal transport, an imagistic seepage:
from the caves of Chauvet, Rouffignac, Lascaux, Peche Merle & Niaux,
thundering off the steppes of Asia, from the moors of the British Isles, the marshlands of the Camargue, squalling off the Sahara through simooms of profit and provision, they come
take up residence

Note: In the "Horse" placement, the application "in the temperature of barn" appeared in *Smelling Mary* and is now a component of this enlarged treatment.

transfer heritage & hide
tend to the arithmetic of bone-*durance*
a memorial quiver

    ***

the sea horse mounts the mermaid
merry plunge
                (utterances moulded in what upbringing
is there a mechanism alert as horse
alertness://:ears ... organ disposition

the Panel of Horses in the Chauvet Cave (the cave with images over 30,000 years
old, the oldest known paintings in the world)
four horse heads stacked on the diagonal[13]
        [Q. It's been said you're a misanthrope, is it true you don't like humanity?
        A. Not at all, I love humanity, ... I just can't find any.]
heads soaking with a humanity that predate homo sapiens & which will antedate
homo sapiens. By "humanity" we mean the emotional empathic, the tenderness
ranges, we mean breeze-mixing & splendiferous co-alightments, we mean
recognition more than endeavor. Did these horses emerge from rock, massaged
forth by some celestial sorcerer, or were they placed there, laid to rest from
millenniums of exhaustive labor, these chaperones of the mythic now lazing &
mellow, grazing among the rock-pastures.

the need to reallocate territory
to chamber a domain &
trot it forward

barn: a recruitment center to insure perpetuity
a holdout against evolution's exclusivity, its disallowance of retreat ...
this conference center schedules to resist the vanishing, dedicates to shape, to
perpetuating configuration ...
the abyss—a de-shapement, an utter dis-figurement, the realm of no corners ...
is the abyss the theater of disappearance

---

[13] These horses can be viewed in *Dawn of Art: The Chauvet Cave,* Harry N. Abrams, New
York, 1996, photo #51 ("the four horses in perspective"), p.68.

a monstrosity of vacuity ...
with no shape can we speak of an impulse, a charge ... perhaps, a petulance?
is the music of vanishing Franck, Satie, Rachmaninoff, ... Little Walter

***

human intercourse with the horse is daylit
the barn activates at night
pitches
sessiles in shrouds of oneiric black
prickling over fallen pasture lands
mists burin an etymology of herd
hoof, stalwart & emblematic, flags a species
swathes an indigenity, gathers
surreption,
arises as a ghost chorus from a long buried
reverberative, munitioning
muzzles
eco-caustic & overdue ...
sizzling spits
of
recalcitrant heat

in the hull of bareback

lingering smoke from a retrolingual squall
scrambling grammar perfervid
tambourine smacking imps outwitting the oversized

through a prehistoric snorkeling subdividing breath
the
New Speech
speaking of augment & wander
bristling new harmonies in the dark ear of the crow
measuring panther by wind

across this salinity divide
hide strophing the great white of the plains
banking to the breeze of an incalculable wonder
an eruption of tone resembling a maturating pinto
a stride like an ancient command
repeating

EXCORIATE EXHALE: ROUTING SOUTINE

(for Clayton Eshleman, Esti Dunow, & Maurice Tuchman

hurl cyclonic pigment dressage drugged passeriform multi-dimensional
splendiferous fest
impastoed lachrymal boulder-blush boucle-heaves bully the decimal
annunciation is culpable matter
time   an event or a consideration
        "Soutine & Modern Art" at the Cheim & Reade Gallery, NYC, Summer
2006, & Soutine
this Surge this packed voltaic scintillator leaps the wall reestablishes & invents
connectivities *creates* worlds dwarfs adjacencies & why … the mind-spite of "why,"
the need for explanation, to penetrate the igneous mute, to volunteer rabbit fur …
what about this tortured (tortured as in tortuous with roundabouts, switchbacks,
manic cyclings) intensity possesses, resists restrictions, demoniacally assaults,
coagulates into ether & substance, explodes expansionist sprawl past galleries &
modernists to transplant & implant,—to *Brand!*
to impugn, to … erode boundaries & barriers to paint past the substance of
painting – is all art in flight from its instrumentation? – brush dabs = darts drilling
into the cosmos a psychic liasoning upswelling/underwelling the soil a robust
Whitman relish-cock splurge peregrinate fertilizations – Rimbaud's: "a poetic
language accessible some day to all the senses" – in "View of Cagnes" the tilt to the
right to launch to rocket-fire, the tension in the homes that of sprinters crouched
in racing start poised to uncoil, the homes at any moment set to unwind & sprint
into the hills, this "unsettlement" not as disarray but as heightened preparation,
Transition-Divinized, … *Mobilization*
there is, here, a suggestibility (an argument?) that the thing painted, known to us
as the tree, hill, house, exists in structure as a makeshift-energy-collection capable
at any moment of redirecting this energy into an alterior formulation, there is a
constant reminder not to get too comfortable, to appreciate form as flux, as the
gratuitous designatory …
                foul   flower   fruit   fish
                f-u-s-e-d
values democratized
matter pulverized
the trophy wall non-bankable

entire canvases gasping

form into form   the "Great Pheasant" & bed bleed into one another   reds
unreconciled   inter-transpicuous object-flushing
the forks in "Rabbit With Forks" anthropomorphize, no, they don't
"anthropomorphize" because the human is not attributed, it's already there, welling
out of psyche, boundaries that say "this is this & that is that" blur, the fork is a
human digit is a fork, the fork has hunger is enlivened with sensate, uni-Versal be-
STirment, objects = arousal functions, vulva factions, the fork-digits tingling with
appetite, poised to devour ...

breeding image hives hybridizing consequences still-dwelling in our windows-to-be-
born[14]

in the serpentine "Still Life with Fish" the mouth gasps, we hear the gasp, a never-
before-formulated other-worldly tone, life crunching out a divinely reeded exhale,
departure points quivering at the border lands, "the dead forms as vigorous on the
slanting table as in their wild existence under water."[15]

        no silence in his pictures, the table & carcasses dialogue, robustly intermingle ...
blend   this is a painter who expurgates dualism   an optic sub-mariner
        a perceptual geothermal steam vent prospering hyperdimensional
Godwinian politics,[16]
this is to say that for Soutine – *Agitation*
Soutine wrote:
"Once I saw the village butcher slice the neck of a bird & drain the blood out of it.
I wanted to cry out, but his joyful expression caught the sound in my throat. This
cry, I always feel it there. When, as a child, I drew a crude portrait of my professor,
I tried to rid myself of this cry, but in vain. When I painted the beef carcass it was
still this cry that I wanted to liberate. I have still not succeeded."

Soutine is the Anti-Kosher pouring the blood back to the animal, the violent phys-
icality he employed "banging" at the canvas, a child's beseechment – invigorated by

---

[14] Riffing on lines from Clayton Eshleman's "Soutine's Lapis" in *From Scratch,* Black Sparrow Press,
      Santa Rosa, 1998, p. 88.

[15] Monroe Wheeler, *Soutine.*

[16] After William Godwin.

the adult's strength of limb – to "let live," that *catch-in-the-throat* to change the world, the butcher's joy of slaughter obviating expression, intercession, ,, tame solutions, the errant magnanimous ...

maturity is man submitting to the condition of man   Soutine never grew up, Artists never grow up, reconciliation is a password to the status quo ... who among us feels his cry, who among us has lost his swallow .....

Soutine is lousy with liveliness, turban-swirling love, death-evaporative, to paint like Soutine is to evaporate death is to call into question the very meaning & category of death, other than in its quotidianized & provincialized form death doesn't exist, to be told that which shapes so much of our lives doesn't exist is to experience metamorphosis, is to become pigment & light, to become lemon glow & hibiscus, canasta green & rummy incarnadine, it's to be simultaneously aerial & marine, finger & claw, it's to understand refrigeration as prayer meeting, it's to be a burning ember ported on the wing of a Mongolian Eagle,—
"To love is to will the self-fulfillment of the beloved, & to find, in the very activity of loving, an incidental but vitalizing increase of oneself."[17]

His eye bloomed the lit-upon   a roast-fest of optical opulence
                    Orgiastic Seeing
          a shamanic priapus invigorating matter
To remove or extinguish what his perception en-*dowed* was to decrease his self. It was akin to a personal assault, to nullify what his eye had emblazoned with fire ...

Death violates Soutine's still life, for Soutine a still life is a study in the un-stilled, the non-programmable, those nuggets refusing retardation, unlike in Rilke's requiem, Soutine is unwilling to let his models water, to unravel *his* making, there is no "setting it all in order is the task *we* have continually before us," this—this art—is not an equal opportunity employer, it is fierce will, resurrecting environment to satisfy sensibility, to the extent that (according to the legend) "when the glorious colors of the flesh of the steer were hidden from the enthralled gaze of the painter by an accumulation of flies, he paid a wretched little model to sit beside it & fan them away," Not to obscure—but, to Reveal—"anything in this dimension" Not as Rilke says to "transform these things, they aren't real, they are only the reflections upon the polished surface of our being," because "these things" are the Only Real! in fact, not real enough 'cause not seen *enough,* seeing is impoverished,

---

[17] Olaf Stapledon

has been besieged with sterility, to permit the see-er to SEE, to penetrate to interior necessity, vacuitous void, porous oblong, vacuumed bedrock, to seethe with life – an interior susurration gilded with imaginal radiance ...

There is a state of death so zany with eccentricity that it bullies life. It shames the life out of life with its instructions on liveliness.

Soutine pierces Death & emerges on the other side, where like the Rilkean Angel capable of unconditional feeling, there is no stifle no termination point there is the fusion of feeling & eternality, the abolishment of the shamefully temporal, the joltingly transitory & the blasphemous static ... & so objects fuse, merge into one another, as the Great Pheasant & Bed bleed together, a porous duet, spirits intermingling, corrupt with influence ...

Animalia

The animals he chose, – Medusa-writhing from his abdomen, bellying out of
cavity pit,—eatables, staples in the carnivore diet, he chose them? or they emerged,
wringing through his psyche to sponge out everyman's carnivore complex, a
routing as perturbation, as the perambulatory inviolate...
all art is a means for ordering affliction, for assigning chaos,
& "affliction," as in stricken with, overwhelmed, invaded, impregnated with
alien...
my thesis: Soutine is an abdominal artist painting from nervous indigestion, "He
always suffered from chronic nervous indigestion."[18] He went on to die on August
9, 1943 from stomach ulcers. The majority of animals he addresses are for the
belly – digestibles; I imagine his own body splaying open like the "Carcass of Beef"
with his intestines unraveling into vacuum-like hoses like those Hollywood Alien
movies where wet vile inventions concocted to revile burst from the stomach flap-
ping & wriggling voraciously, rapacious for prey, Soutine born empty, Soutine the
everyman empty, Promethean defiance, in place of empty – fire, the unfailing vigor
of appetite, to never know the comfort of "fill," a convulsive refusal to dwell any-
where but in the essentially vitalistic, a SCORCH! combusting circumference ...

Why artists choose the animals they choose? Or are they chosen, by the animal,
a person = an animal(s) composite, ... I propose to transmigrate the psychic-
animal,—paradoxically, & opposing my thesis, the one horse I see of Soutine's is a
sway-back droop of an animal, an insufficiency destined for earth swallow—upon
reflection I reconsider, the vitality is *not* absent from the horse, it is just not located
in the corpus of the horse, unlike the "Carcass of Beef" swarming with visceral-
colossicity, the energy system in "The Horse" forfeits the locus of vitality from the
existent to the abstractly conceptual, in this case to *decay,* to the inevitable annul-
ment of the temporal animal, to that magnetically powerful earth-drag comman-
deering the animal downward...

I supplement Soutine's beef & foul with Franz Marc's horses, I invoke a quicken-
ing: I implant Franz Marc's "The Small Yellow Horses"—these horses are nothing
but liveliness & hind, a canvas of ensorcelling seductivities – I loose these beauties
on Soutine's "View of Cagnes," I place them about ⅘ down the canvas, on the road

---

[18] Monroe Wheeler, *Soutine,* P.42

across from the bottommost house, slowly they uncoil, the two forefront horse's
heads on the diagonal, heads that could be magnificent emblazonings on a
shamanic spear, a whinny to their right, manes flag, the third horse turns left to
contact their inquisition, symbols of feline grace & celestial purr these bodies
morph from Grecian-smooth to rippling delineation, sinew & muscle, rib & flesh
pronounce, they rear & tuck, snort & wheeze, they are tremulous & cyclonic, I
color the horses alizarin, turmeric, & gold, I paint their heads fuchsia, manganese,
& goethite, I run pinstripes of turquoise, viridian, & sepia down their rumps, then
scarlet, topaz, & mauve, I turn their tails umber, periwinkle, & brown, also scarlet,
pumpernickel, & sage—I remove all the other paintings from the wall & magnify
"View of Cagnes" ten times – the houses gape & agitate, reacting to the flurrying
fund of hoof frenzy before them like witnessing a conductor with St. Vitus's dance,
the horses return to all fours, prance & circle, quivering with titillation & novelty,
horse & house advance – hide & home, skin & mortar – sniff one another, manu-
facture airs, horse/home/road/hill, a quartet
charging for redemption

Color

Not in any formalized sense, no laconic breakdown, no tri-partite divisions of hue/luminosity/intensity, but color as activity & contagion, as arousal mannerisms & vowel sounds percolating pigment flirtation migratory bemusement ladder, color as jealousy & lachrymose, as cereal & crust, color building chordal blocks & agricultural progressions irrigation by-ways autumnal bridle paths Ferris wheels gypsy copulatives & bulldozer, color to sleep in to love in, to frost to suck, color as intimacy & reproach, as unreliable navigator & sleuth, a lexiconic hydra, a beetle, a moth, an invitation experiencing mechanical failure, & *the call of color is to color where color fails,* to uncover the undercover of cover, to reset the receptors, to board phantom wavelengths & establish cherish, to remonstrate the idolatrous zigzag of supra-retinal perceptual frolic...

Letter

Dear Soutine,

You can't know how I've struggled to write this, how the intimacy of our con-
nection seems to violate conventional modes, ... so why am I writing this? for the
sake of the poem? no, the poem is to consume you like the beef & foul you lay out,
the poem is to hang you like a rabbit from the rafters, or stretch you on a table with
the forks of my hunger lusting to sink your flesh to taste you, to swill you in my
mouth. You see how content humans look when they masticate, perhaps that is one
of the few times other than expellment that they flirt with satisfaction, is that why
they've pushed us to the margins? to the outskirts where we can be manageable? so
we will fail to threaten their domestic blisses, their cherished comfort stations? you
know we do that, Soutine, we have to face up to our effects, the "affective imponder-
ables," we can't be harsh & self-pitying when we come to terms with the discomfort
we cause, pinging like black hail off their stale palates. To meet in this vector blind
the way we have is to dispel men from their duck hunts, is to deprive them of their
camouflage. It is to inform congregations how powerless they are to stall the inven-
tion of new universes, the advancement of hirsute guitars. Our purpose was never
to hurt, but to *move,* to rattle them out of their stasis, we were both small & vulnera-
ble as children, beaten by older brothers, we both knew tremendous cruelty, how the
diminished went unprotected, were place mats for other's venom, so we were
pushed around & excluded, but we never caved, ... how could we, tossing with
seizures, under phantom-arrest with a foreign & superior hemoglobin, we've devel-
oped no taste for other things, consumed as we are with the great matters we have
no tolerance for golf or spectatorship, we greet our contemporaries as so many
passers by, I have waited long for a friend like you, someone I could bank on... for
understanding, for the soothe of correspondence, or as I felt years ago in Paris when
I wrote —

In The Cimitiere De Montparnasse There Are No Dead

> I go to Vallejo, to Beckett, to Baudelaire, thirteen years old & reading *Les
> Fleurs du mal,* my pube patch just forming with that soft delicacy of early
> curl, imagery curling through the enterprise of my imagination, & when a
> crowd gathers around Baudelaire I await their dispersal, I want to go one
> on one... Root to Root...

Bau-de-laire, Good friend, old buddy, I come to you, in midlife... all of us now – Sartre, Beckett, me, you, assuaged of years, galloping the prairies of free form, detachments of vigorous infuriations slapping the universe awake, what stirred us above all if not the corpses the unenlightened the daily excruciations of numbness throttling our urgency to invigorate... loom monolithic tombstones flame alive
more individual than the strollers walling 5ᵗʰ avenue the Champs Elysees Rodeo Drive, more life quivering through the rocks of the institute of death than all the human cargo freighting the freeways buses metros aircraft boulevards & avenues tired soul-slabs slopping over the high rises of the world spluttering to their decimation...—

We're fortunate to have each other, Chaim, I first saw you in Paris, & I was excited, & certainly more than moved, but I wasn't *devoured,* not as I am now, I even saw you in 1995 at the Jewish Museum in NYC & was thrilled, agitated, but not devoured... & why is that Chaim?, you haven't changed, & I can't use cheap expressions & say "I've matured" because that will tell us nothing, if anything, it seems I've become more wounded, more vulnerable, existing in a state of perpetual grief, for the butcheries are daily & ever more exaggerated, with the butchers having no remorse, they gloat audibly over their latest slaughters, so that... – each day more of me is sliced open, I am a carcass that breathes – *a respirating corpse* – ... I can't go shopping... I'm a bit choked up now, Chaim, but more later...

Supplemental Insert

Informed that the Barnes Foundation in Merion, Pa. has the largest collection of Soutines in America, &, additionally, that the Foundation is terminal & at some point in the near future will be assembled under different auspices, I make plans to witness the collection as Barnes envisioned.

Doctor Barnes put Soutine on the map; he also rescued him from penury. Soutine's dealer, Zborowski, was despairing over carrying Soutine for so long with no pay off, that, after a quarrel with his wife, he "took a batch of Soutine's pictures, stripped them off their sub-frames, rolled up the lot & shoved them in the kitchen stove to burn them." &, as Zborowski related to Marevna, "The next day – just listen to this – suddenly I get a visit from the famous American collector, Dr. Barnes, who just happens to be passing through Paris. 'What have you got that's new? Show me,' he says, & I show him Kislings, Modiglianis & so on. '& what's this?' he asks, pointing to a little Soutine on the wall. 'Oh,' I say, 'it's by some wretched Russian.' 'Bring it to the light,' he says, & examines it from all angles. 'Any more like these?' he asks. 'Yes,' I say, 'just wait a moment, I'll run across to a friend who has some.' Then I dash to the kitchen in a cold sweat, wondering if the cook's burned up the pictures or not. I open the stove – thank God, no! Wonderful! I heat the iron & iron out a few creases through a cloth, & then I produce a living soul for this American – not my own soul, you understand, but Soutine's."[19]

Barnes bought everything & put Soutine under employment.

This precipice, the fragility of direction – the canvases about to be burned versus the canvases saved & injected into the art world to go forever *burning*. Art to ignite & salvage, to *cleanse*.

I visit the Barnes Foundation. Dr. Barnes launched his financial empire by introducing a new antiseptic silver compound to the marketplace. He also launched Soutine into the market place. I see Dr. Barnes as the inter-transpicuous contiguous trans-mundane medicinal provider. A Doctor introducing antiseptic in both pharmaceutical & artistic formulations. This notion of Art as curative, as medicinal, is often overlooked, & the manner in which Art performs medicinal functions is, properly, the province of a separate study. But, while running the risk of "short shrift," I will suggest some indicators. The mental & the physical suffer equally from clotting, arterial blockage, constriction, fattiness, & atrophy if not attended to properly, if permitted to wallow in desuetude. Strategies for bodily repair

---

[19]   Marevna, *Life With the Painters of La Ruche,* P.152.

normatively fall under the headings of diet & exercise. We can apply those same categories to improve our mental health. The mind, like the body, needs to be exercised in the plastically-elongatory-ameliorative, trotted out to the training fields, & what is fed to the mind as nourishment – diet (i.e. classic literature versus television soaps) – will effect one's mental hygiene. & just as one must *train* one's body to achieve a superlative state of fitness, so Art can provide the "weight" training necessary to improve & tone our mental musculature. It is an invitation to participate in the sensorially procreant ecstatically perceptual perpetual tingle. In the words of Doctor Barnes, "The artist must open our eyes to what unaided we could not see..."[20]

---

[20] Albert C. Barnes, *The Art In Painting,* p. 3.

Slam Incunabula

My fifth visit to the Cheim & Reade gallery is on a day of rain & dark omen. This day I find myself rooted to the main gallery, unable to detach myself. Particularly I am grabbed by the landscapes, the cumulous skylight casts a devil-blue, yellowing the electric lights, the whites become more vivid, & perhaps due to a compound-ment of visits, the landscapes claw into me more ferociously than ever, a rare pri-vacy accompanies this claw, the depth of the claw annulling the gallery walkers, placing the landscapes along private places in my interior where they can't be spotted, I triangulate between "View of Cagnes," "Landscape at Ceret," & "Land-scape with Trees," providentially the rain thickens, & the percussive popping upon the plastic skylight becomes Art Blakey in "Night in Tunisia," drums, cymbals & maracas intersect the rhythms of the landscapes, the rhythms intermingle & enlarge, the main gallery sizzles in polyrhythmic glow, in bombinative surplus –
I saw Blakey before he died at the Catalina Bar & Grill, as a kid I followed him, to see him live was a gift, his smile & white teeth, his teeth plastering the homes in Cagnes, him propelling the band, perpetually propulsing, he died a week after I saw him, but I don't believe it, it's not what I'm hearing –
a whirling wailing Dolphy-esque trio – body/canvases/rain – whorling in newly bred intimacies, rocketed to a rarefied ether orb rotational calendrics
—phantasmagoria clutch egret storms slam incunabula—

& I note that each landscape has a road, a road for each landscape has landscapes road a, the road to less road, the road to more road,[21] I ponder road as routing, then change my direction & understand road as rhythm, a tympanic surge chunked out of earth,
the road paces & unwinds as a top hurled from a string,
road as peristaltic bass, a dragon tail
flashing whippy geologies

caffeinated on landscape I retreat from the trilogy, pass De Kooning's "Untitled 11" 1978 which, adjacent to "View of Cagnes," is so quashed that it appears a flamboyant amateur guilty of overcivilized posturing, floundering in an inept

---

[21] See Heller Levinson's, *Smelling Mary*

236

pugilism; I approach "Rabbit" 1918 which baffled me last visit because this was the only painting without *Stir,* Soutine was all about agitation & this rabbit looked peaceful, at rest, harmonious...

but today, no, I have wised up, I see him as playing possum, in a state of "pause," I detect a smirk around the lips, a "who are you kidding," this rabbit no longer disputes the exhibition which declares domesticity illusionistic, the rabbit winks, nibbles the green bedding, scampers off...

back under the skylight the percussion pounds, I can't help but move, I dance, facing "Trees At Auxerre" I see gathering, I see cyclonic sweep-up, I see vital elements wrapping into an ancient tribal gourd rattling feverish oblations, I turn to look at "Landscape at Ceret," the trees become spindly Ethiopian dancers charged with divinized elasticity, this isn't just Ethiopia it's Malaga it's Seville it's Mauritania it's Berlin it's Sao Paolo & Pakistan it's Columbia & Kazakhstan, it's marimba & gong, conga & tympani, tom tom & flute, this is geology time zone genome & constitution, foreheads & abdominals, writhing in twists of circumambulatory lunge broadcast cliff syndrome, bluffs of undermine dedicated to reconstitute, arousal orthodoxies notwithstanding wrath-wringing infuriations spin infectious pleas for polite oxygen, for communal belly laughter...

Quotidian Cancel

Again rain. My final visit to this exhibit. It is day sad-saturant. A displacement. A disqualification of the quotidian. Budge refusal. Herbivorous dirge. Lamentation. I dial-in on "View of Cagnes," the attraction (attachment?) is sub-logical, pre-Saharan, it stings like a rum ocean, like a bay on fire, it is time to give back, we are not alone, ... while facing "View of Cagnes" I take a deep breath than exhale my first line,
"hurl cyclonic pigment dressage drugged passeriform multi-dimensional splendiferous   fest..."
the population recedes, encouraged by our solitude, I deliver the second line more robustly,
"impastoed lachrymal boulder-blush boucle-heaves bully the decimal..."
hallowed sunrises warp in a sully of fruit trees, impoverishment slouches to a surly dawn, Soutine's visage issues from the bowels of Cagnes, the grave creases in his face ease into a sturdy smile, my lines stir him, he connects, he is grateful I have come, he thanks me for the letter, we talk, two guys who didn't hitch to any spectacle but that of their own devisement, we are comfortably complicit, hammocking in soul-drench, we chat of small matters, of shoes & weather & edibles, the large matters mushroom unannounced from our persons, from our dedications, with no need for fanfare,—*vibrating revolutionary tusks*—he advises me not to fret the maggot-fests before he departs....

His disappearance empties me of giddy, I amble now, stroll the still-lifes, not wanting to look too intently, preferring to remain in touch with the event of Soutine's departure than with opening fresh visual provocations... I meander the fowl, & again observe how their mouths vibrate holler, expound abyssal recriminations, novels would fail to express the peels of vitriol & pathos orally churning... discussing Excoriate Exhale with Victoria Ganim who directed me to the Peritoneum: "For the most part all our guts lie within this peritoneal bag. The outer peritoneum forms the real skin of the abdominal cavity. The liver, the gut, & the spleen sink into the peritoneal bags & they are all attached to the diaphragm & thus, your breathing has a direct effect on your digestive organs. So if we breathe correctly & deeply the organs are getting a therapeutic massage each time we inhale & exhale. I bet Soutine didn't breathe correctly."[22] The breath & what conditions

---

[22]   Victoria Ganim is a Movement Therapist.

the breath. What breathes through the enterprise of breathing. The climate & the psychically climactic, the soma & the geo-topographical, renditions of "being-in-the world." I consider collapse & routing, if the two congregate or displace one another, clearly the apogee of route is collapse, as conclusion is peak circumcision, routing refutes terminal circumvention, the summarily conclusive, the urge, then, to route is profound & survivalistic & bares circumference as it pertains to enhancing the vigor of exotic Lepidoptera; who can refute that a rational assessment of history spells tragic, not withstanding Bach & Clementine...

So, it is to be my last day & I don't feel any closer to resolving the inquiry that sparked this investigation – the "why" of Soutine's power. If anything, I feel further away, & yet more at ease, immersed in Soutine for two months, rather than feeling a need to explain his power I am enlarged from breathing his power, from Peritoneum-Washing, the need to declare & conjugate, to submit to a quantitative orchestration, no longer seems appropriate or valid, it is like trying to explain origins, the origin of the universe, the origin of myth, there will be theories & confutations of theories but there will be nothing absolute, nothing we can be certain of, this urge to seek origins is itself a subject worthy of investigation, what is the need that impels us to identify an origin? Will it serve to orient us more accurately to where we already are? Preparing to depart, I feel that my non-answer satisfies, & I wish to preserve this sense of resolution, not to poke around trying to define the power of Soutine, I am now comforted with being empowered by Soutine, the capacity of Art to empower, to invigorate & enlarge, is perhaps the appropriate area for investigation, not to disembowel an Artist in the hopes of discovering a Truth-Morsel, but to luxuriate in the ineffable in art, the effluent mystery of creation...

I am at the portal which entrances into the main gallery & there by absentee ballot is The Page Boy at Maxim's, he stands there with his hand outstretched, just like in the painting, & I view that painting *not* to be a "servile" study in the ordinary sense of demeanment, for this page boy is Soutine himself, enthroned in uniform because he serves but *one* master & that master is Art, the artist is a chameleon suiting up for the occasion, as Keats says, "A poet [read painter/artist] is the most unpoetical of anything in existence; because he has no Identity – he is continually in for – as filling some other Body – The Sun, the Moon, the Sea & Men & Women who are creatures of impulse are poetical & have about them an unchangeable attribute – the poet has none; no identity – he is certainly the most unpoetical of all God's Creatures." How resonant that Soutine, uniformed in the Sartrean "in-itself," is there to see me off, with his hand magnified, palm encircled, he is pleading for that breakthrough, that chance, unexpected tip to the insight-sweetspot that will enable him to extend his parameter, to penetrate further, the bituminous eye pits wearied & blistering, puckering from the already-performed excavations, the right shoulder raised aggressively, sharp, angulated, positioning the entire arm-hand into a shovel-complex devoted to digging up exalted divinations... then, as my foot lifts to exit, there is a slight up-jerk to his hand & I take it, I take his cry he couldn't get out, I take this churning aggravation, this squawking squalor scream out into the street, &, with excruciating wringings, offer it here.....

Appendix I[23]

Hinge Theory Diagnostic

(Whereby the operations of Hinge are inspected in the construct "with insinuation," p. 243.)

We will designate the first three encounters with "with insinuation" the Pivot, the Particle, and the Postulate (the 3 P's).

"With" is the pivot whose function is to spring (to unleash, to unmoor) the particle (in this case, "insinuation") into a climate of free fall and unpredictability. And by free fall, we mean that we are liberating the particle from its normative, conventional context and tossing it into question. It might land anywhere and to any effect. "Insinuation" is emboldened to flag this as the element being sprung.[24] The grammatical devices following "insinuation" are the comma and the ellipsis. The comma serves to create a pause and the ellipsis indicates that the particle is adjusting to another climate. We are "hinging" into a new opening. The use of alternative punctuation, say, using a semicolon or a dash, would frame differing results for the postulate. When the reader becomes conversant with the way the punctuation behaves, similar to how a conductor interprets the dynamics in a score, they will be alert as to how the postulate is being rendered. The postulate, "nuance," settles "insinuation" and initiates one's intimacy with the word. We need not ask "with insinuation, What?" We are told. With insinuation, nuance. We are made aware that we are not in any pejorative atmosphere, there is no hint of the derogatory tone that is often associated with "insinuation," it is signaled that "insinuation" will be *growing* in a different direction as we roam "insinuation's" more artful attributes. We are Orienteering. The use of the word "nuance" after the word "insinuation" reinforces the notion of artfulness by allowing

---

23   Appendix I first appeared in *Smelling Mary,* published by Howling Dog Press.

24   We chose the preposition "with" in this volume because of the plethora of intrigue; we could have a parallel set of poems using another preposition, such as "into" — into ... insinuation — though differing unfoldings would result, as every preposition contains an intrinsic value, just as every musical key has its own colorations and soundings.

the participant/practitioner/reader to bathe in the sensual, musical properties of alliteration issuing from the repetition of the "nua" in both words and in the "g(s)lide" of the relaxed sibilant "ce" sound after the "ins" and "tion" sound. It's as if (in a very magical and haunting way), "nuance" was delivered *from* "insinuation;" there's something very visceral and powerful in this suggestion – the postulate being *born-out-of* the particle. The following line and words (glide and slide) are a fleshing out of the artful aroma issuing from "insinuation." The construction "g(s)lide" is an example of Hinge operating in a single word. Installation of the (s) indicates that the word has dual functions fused into one transmission. The word "glide" is both glide and slide, they are interchangeable and flippable. It is both glide and slide working independently, as well as being compacted together into "glideslide." The imaginative participant, seeing the parenthetical (s) as flotational, may also choose to attach the "s" to the end of the word to form "glides" and "slides," thus opening up a third-dimensional function. The following words and lines (the catapult throning/to spring/novelty/palomino curvatures) serve to acclimate (to insinuate to the participant) the context in which "insinuation" has landed. "Insinuation" is being rhapsodized, this is the turn "insinuation" has taken, "the catapult throning" implies that the apparatus (catapult) for hurling/launching is being enthroned, placed in a position of admiration; indeed, the whole Hinge mechanism (the three P's) can be seen as having glided and slid into a mechanism that thrusts it outward, tosses it forward to novelty, to feast on the subtle marvels of "palomino curvatures." We have swung away from brash overtures, from braggadocio, from the merely outspoken, and are feasting on the "combinatory bonanzas," the "arousal pits," that "insinuation" can deliver/bestow; we are given opportunities to open the door of the word and experience its greater vistas, to see how the evenly divided tail of the fish ("homocercal symmetries") can insinuate a symmetrical universe. "Squid festoons" is an image of squids forming a festoon, as well as insinuating "squid" as a verb which, by virtue of their movement quality, have the ability to create or eject a festoon. The ://: device is intended to suggest "squid festoons" seesawing with "roam mollusk." "Roam mollusk" operates multiply. "Roam" can serve as an adjective identifying the type of mollusk we are dealing with—one that *roams*—or as a verb inviting us to roam the mollusk, to caress the smooth hard shell, as well as to probe the soft underbelly. The last three lines could be a mission statement for Hinge Theory. "In the depositories of tale," in the mythic wellsprings of story, formations are lurching forward to be discovered and addressed; we need only apply attention ("periscope heed") to open the door.

The diagnostician wishes from his inspection that the participants' association (intimacy, relationship) with the word "insinuation" should be vaster, more charged. The word "insinuation" should have amassed more Volume. It is a function of Hinge Theory to vitalize language, to insinuate more splendor.

A hallmark of Hinge is its propagatory nature. It resembles cellular reproduction in its capacity to spin off and multiply. Components in a Mobile Probe Collective[25] lust to be addressed, yearn to be spurred into free fall. In "with insinuation", "roam" was just begging for it. Therefore, "with roam" was snapped into the Hinge shuttle and was sprung. With Hinge, we live in a universe of Flow Throughs, with "withs" connecting to other "withs," with "withs" connecting to "roads" and "roads" to "smellings" and "smellings" to "withs" and with "withs" and "roads" and "smellings" intermingling with the latest Vehicular Structure "in the __ of __," which will *fuse* with those ever-omnicropping Dehiscent Agitators yet to be born. Hinge is a perpetual interconnecting profusely propagatory contagiously enlivening multi-universe of multi-complementary extensions.

WITH

INSINUATION, ... nuance
g(s)lide the catapult
throning   to
spring   novelty   palomino
curvatures   stun
convexities   arousal pits
homocercal symmetries
squid festoons ://: roam mollusk
combinatory bonanzas
in the depositories of tale
lurch formations
periscope heed

---

25 *Mobile Probe Collective:* Also known as MUPAEs—Mutational Update Panel Animation Extenders.

APPENDIX II

Cogitation Upon ://*:*

The symbol :*//*: is employed to suggest a seesawing between the words surrounding it.—A Crisscrossery Flexion. In the application "with assembly" (see below) the seesaw activity of "crisscrossery & settlement" and "accumulation & mass" throw off differing characteristics. With C&S, there is an interplay between intense activity (the neologism "crisscrossery" is intended to suggest a high-caliber activity, perhaps a frenzy) and repose ("settlement"), thus, a going up/a going down, oppositional placements.

A&M, on the other hand, is more relational than oppositional. We are not dealing with a *tension,* but a *conductivity.* Accumulation may result in mass, and mass can be seen as a collected accumulation.

We are considering :*//*: to indicate that it does not denote strict valuations—one seesawing episode may be tense while another may be harmonious—but, rather, exposes the *inter-play* between the players, the *frisson.* It is a *springboard* for rapport. And, like persons, the words rapporting in seesaw each have their own dispositions, their own organic personalities.

WITH

ASSEMBLY, ...　　gathering
pieces　　　　put　　　　　　ensembling
　　　　conferential
cohabitation　　　　　　crisscrossery://:settlement
　　　　equitation
acquisition & divestiture
accumulation://:mass
the mockery of pit
paucity blush harborage the pilfer sturdy if misleading
climate is an aggregate is a theater for sound
hauling is a bringing to
construction: anatomical self-expression
leaving well enough alone

Appendix III

ZAPs

The ZAP, a Zinging Activiation Procedure, is a long, large mouth/lung full of a legato one breath fractally collusional line intended to *de*-stabilize & to evoke (not to claim) alterior reassemblies. The line has the responsibility of shattering/exploding (in this function, military language, such as "missiles" and "neutron bombs" designed to penetrate the toughest armor, is not entirely off the mark, save for the fact that ZAPs are more of a *fertility attack* than an annihilation) static, conventional, stale, & inhibiting formulations. From the breakdown(through), pluralistic oscillating fragile marvels emerge. We seek to replace the automatic/automatous link-clicking-compartmentalized-meaning-conditioned-mentally-sclerotic landscape with one of the continuously erupting Miraculous.

Below, we will submit a line in an attempt to shed insight on the nature of ZAPs. The line we will examine is from the poem "Coconut Vulva" (*Toxicity,* HDP. 2005, page 10) and is:

> "your strawberry-muffler breasts porcine valve distribution coiffed enzyme wash..."

Now, if you asked me after a public reading what this meant, I would have to say that I couldn't give an answer on the spot, I'd have to take a moment to recreate it; my words are never haphazard or nonsensical, they are thoughtfully composed, and, if they come unannounced or spontaneously, they must bear up to my further scrutiny to see if they *serve* the poem. So I take this line, which has, for me, such a virile psychic claw, and decide to examine it in terms of "meaning"—a term, by the way, I am coming more and more to loathe, because what this culture means by "meaning," I find (for the most part) *meaningless.* Donning my analytical cap, I see breasts being rhapsodized, placed in curious contradistinctions, amid the succulence of a strawberry and the throaty functions of a muffler, even compared to a pig, which might seem outlandish unless one considers the nutritional value of a pig, the compact contours of a pig, the sloshing mud-caking sensual properties that pigs are often aligned with (kids playing with mud pies, laughing when they see pigs, etc.), so now I not only see breasts differently and more expansively, I am also deriving new associations from and about pigs and mufflers, each image is integrating and cross-territorializing with the other, then to "valve distribution" which kicks off from "porcine" so one can connect "porcine" to "valvular systems," as well as breasts to valves, in terms of nutritional distribution, essential supply, lubricious machinery, and, again, the fleshifying of machinery and vice versa, which, for me, creates a sensual complex, all deftly topped by "coiffed enzyme wash"; "coiffed" takes the former words and elicits an insouciant domesticity, a sort of luxuriating charm, giving the former images an "enzyme wash" do (hairdo), the whole resulting in an intestinal cleansing, a psychic rinse.

This leads me to simile, which I pretty much abhor—I may have used it twice in the last ten years, and primarily in prose where I will start the sentence with "Like"—and Metaphor, which is from the Greek word for *transfer,* which I like, but which I try to do in a new way, since I want something even more intense and intermingling than traditional metaphor so I do away with the conventional links and stockpile image upon image, "muffler breasts porcine valve," thereby hoping to mangle, mingle, and jolt our perceptual apparatus into new (fresh) formulations, or, one could see it as an attempt to permanently Mobilize formulations so that they avoid sclerosis.

Professor Mary Newell, who has taken an interest in my work, terms this component of my poetry, that is, the so-called dense line, the "ZAP", as "Fractal Collusion."

Now, here's the rub, and for me, the most important point: all the above is the *least* important aspect of the line, and my singular, quick analysis is only one perspective; hopefully, the line will throw off multiplicitious associations, suggestions, and conjurings; there is, obviously, no One "right" meaning, and the true potency of the line has to do with swallow and imbibation, with viscera; it should be read in one breath in legato, and when you do that, it should feel good in the mouth, feel good to *say,* become a delicious mouthful you enjoy swirling through your cerebral lobes, a line that plasmically circulates, that has an electrical charge to it. Perhaps that is why musicians seem to be my best audience. In a sense, it is pre-cognitive or supra-cognitive.

What I have learned, perhaps, is that there is something beyond sense and nonsense, something we might term NewSense (nusense?); getting away from the demon of Western Dualism, it is necessary to develop alternative strategies to be able to expand further rather than submitting to our cultural conditioning that demands shrivellization.

To the line I examined, which some might charge as "obscure" or "impenetrable," I would submit that it is, rather, exploding with meaning, is shivering with solicitation, is, in fact, a shamanic dervish committed to save us.

This approach summons intellectual intuition, a call to develop the sub- and supra-rational, in Artaud's words, to live in "the realm of the affective imponderable." And again, Artaud, what is called for "is like a supreme reorganization in which only the laws of illogic participate, and in which there triumphs the discovery of a New Meaning."

HELLER LEVINSON's previous books include *Smelling Mary, ToxiCity: Poems of the Coconut Vulva, Alameda, Because You Wanted A Wedding Ring,* and *Another Line.* Levinson originated Hinge Theory, which he envisions as a universal linguistics within applied poetics. His artistic and musical collaborations using Hinge Theory is growing rapidly and widely as its applications in these areas is limitless. Levinson's poems and writings have appeared in hundreds of journals and literary outlets around the world. He lives in New York City where he studies animal behavior. See more at www.hellerlevinson.com.

TITLES FROM BLACK WIDOW PRESS

TRANSLATION SERIES

Approximate Man and Other Writings
by Tristan Tzara. Translated and edited
by Mary Ann Caws.

Art Poétique by Guillevic.
Translated by Maureen Smith.

The Big Game by Benjamin Péret.
Translated with an introduction by
Marilyn Kallet.

Capital of Pain by Paul Eluard.
Translated by Mary Ann Caws,
Patricia Terry, and Nancy Kline.

Chanson Dada: Selected Poems
by Tristan Tzara. Translated with an
introduction and essay by Lee Harwood.

*Essential Poems and Writings of
Joyce Mansour: A Bilingual Anthology*
Translated with an introduction by
Serge Gavronsky.

Essential Poems and Prose of Jules Laforgue
Translated and edited by Patricia Terry.

*Essential Poems and Writings of
Robert Desnos: A Bilingual Anthology*
Edited with an introduction and essay
by Mary Ann Caws.

EyeSeas (Les Ziaux) by Raymond Queneau.
Translated with an introduction by Daniela
Hurezanu and Stephen Kessler.

Furor and Mystery & Other Writings
by René Char. Edited and translated by
Mary Ann Caws and Nancy Kline.

The Inventor of Love & Other Writings by
Gherasim Luca. Translated by Julian and
Laura Semilian. Introduction by Andrei
Codrescu. Essay by Petre Răileanu.

La Fontaine's Bawdy
by Jean de la Fontaine. Translated with
an introduction by Norman R. Shapiro.

Last Love Poems of Paul Eluard
Translated with an introduction by
Marilyn Kallet.

Love, Poetry (L'amour la poésie)
by Paul Eluard. Translated with an essay by
Stuart Kendall.

Poems of André Breton: A Bilingual Anthology
Translated with essays by Jean-Pierre Cauvin
and Mary Ann Caws.

Poems of A.O. Barnabooth by Valéry Larbaud.
Translated by Ron Padgett and Bill Zavatsky.

Preversities: A Jacques Prévert Sampler
Translated and edited by Norman R. Shapiro.

The Sea and Other Poems by Guillevic.
Translated by Patricia Terry. Introduction
by Monique Chefdor.

To Speak, to Tell You?
Poems by Sabine Sicaud. Translated by
Norman R. Shapiro. Introduction and
notes by Odile Ayral-Clause.

forthcoming translations

Essential Poems and Writings of Pierre Reverdy
Edited by Mary Ann Caws. Translated by
Mary Ann Caws, Patricia Terry, Ron Padgett,
and John Ashberry.

A Life of Poems, Poems of a Life by Anna de
Noailles. Translated by Norman R. Shapiro.
Introduction by Catherine Perry.

WWW.BLACKWIDOWPRESS.COM